Praise for 7 Steps to a 720 Credit Score

"Tirone's book is a good overview of protecting and correcting your own credit. Good credit should be guarded by all, especially entrepreneurs. Become and remain bankable!"
—**William H. Crookston**, Ph.D., Professor of Entrepreneurship, University of Southern California

"**7 Steps to a 720 Credit Score** is a clear and powerful process for reinventing oneself financially. It provides motivation for people trying to take control of their financial future. I would like to see all real estate agents read this book both for themselves and their clients."
—**Floyd Wickman**, CSP, CPAE, Speakers Hall of Fame

"The **7 Steps** have changed my life. Years ago, I hit some hard times and ended up with a credit score of 0. Even my own bank refused to give me a secured credit card. Then I read **7 Steps to a 720 Credit Score**. I did everything Philip said. Less than two months later, my score jumped from 0 to 718! Almost overnight, I've gone from not qualifying for a secured card to being less than a year away from a home loan."
—**Tim Michaels**, Santa Monica, CA

"Managing your credit is one of the core secrets of success, which makes **7 Steps** the perfect resource for people who have great credit, bad credit, or no credit at all. Tirone's book teaches you everything you ever needed to know about credit."
—**Jennifer Kushell**, author of the *New York Times* best-seller, *Secrets of the Young & Successful*

"I learned how to increase my credit score from 671 to 758 in just four months. Because of the **7 Steps**, I can now afford a lot more house and keep my payments the same."
—**Andre M. Jones**, North Hills, CA

"With one single step, my highest credit score jumped to 780! Having this made it possible for me to qualify for a low-interest loan for an investment property I just purchased."
—**Kim Davis**, Los Angeles, CA

"As a realtor, I'm responsible for making my clients' dreams come true, and I couldn't do that without the **7 STEPS**. Time and time again, the **7 STEPS** have given my clients the ability to qualify for the best home loans available. In fact, every homeowner, homebuyer, realtor, and mortgage broker in the country needs a copy of **7 STEPS TO A 720 CREDIT SCORE!**"
—**Erik Flexner**, Boardwalk Realty, Los Angeles, CA

"**7 STEPS TO A 720 CREDIT SCORE** really opened my eyes. The book gave me concrete and easy-to-follow advice on how to turn things around. For that alone, it was worth the investment. But the thing that struck me is that Philip really cares. He doesn't just want more business. He genuinely wants to help people repair their credit, buy a home, and get the best rates. I only wish I lived in his area so he could be *my* mortgage broker."
—**Sarah Baker**, Bozeman, MT

"As a result of these simple steps, we raised our scores and secured a 30-year fixed-rate mortgage at 6.5 percent interest, and we were able to get some cash back to do home improvements. The new gas barbeque arrives next week, just in time for some summer grilling!"
—**Steve and Jennifer Goldstein**, Los Angeles, CA

"**7 STEPS** did more than raise my credit score: it changed my lifestyle. As a result of the 160-point jump in my score, I can strengthen my financial portfolio and provide my family with more stability. In fact, I'm flying to Atlanta next week to purchase my first rental property and with my 735 credit score, I can negotiate the lowest interest rates and secure the best terms available."
—**Vance Yetts**, Inglewood, CA

7 STEPS TO A 720™ CREDIT SCORE

Seven Easy Steps to the Ideal Credit Score

THIRD EDITION

7 STEPS TO A 720 CREDIT SCORE / Philip X. Tirone-3rd ed.

ISBN 0-9768656-8-8

TABLE OF CONTENTS

credit
and the american
dream

Consider two people, Mark and Jill. They have the same job, the same income, the same debt, and the same savings, but Mark has poor credit (below a 620 credit score) and Jill has excellent credit (above a 720). Mark and Jill each decide to buy a $333,500 home, both paying $33,350 as a down payment. Let's see how their finances differ over the life of the loan.

Because of his poor credit score, Mark ends up paying about $589 a month more than Jill. That adds up to $127,224 over 18 years. Jill, on the other hand, can use the money she saves because of her good credit on a vacation home, her child's college tuition, and investments. With the proper strategy, this money can double, triple, or even quadruple throughout the course of her lifetime. Fostered by low interest rates and wise investments, Jill has $410,857 in savings (at a 4 percent interest rate) at the end of her 30-year loan. Mark ends up paying $212,040 extra during the same 30 years, and he has almost no money in savings.[1]

Buying a home is the American Dream, the incentive for countless immigrants to flood to the United States in years past, the daydream of the blue-collar worker. And yet in today's market, it seems sadly out of reach for most people, especially in places like California, where the median price paid for a home reached $478,000 in June 2006.[2]

Truth be told, owning a home is not an unattainable dream. In fact, banks are making it easier and easier for people, even those with no credit or bad credit (like Mark), to qualify for home loans. But such loans come with towering interest rates and correspondingly high monthly payments that can turn even a modest American Dream into a nightmare.

What most lenders fail to tell borrowers is that there is a secret, a way to attain the American Dream without paying an arm and a leg. The secret: a high credit score. With a credit score of 720 or above, most lenders ignore the borrower's income and savings. Even someone on a teacher's salary can qualify for the best available loans with the lowest interest rates so long as she has strong credit.

In fact, credit counts for 70 percent of your mortgage application. And 720 is that magic number that will take you 70 percent of your way home.

---

1. Based on January 23, 2005, interest rates. Rates updated daily at www.MyFICO.com.
2. DataQuick Real Estate News, www.DQNews.com, a subsidiary of DataQuick Information Systems, July 20, 2006.

Remember that credit affects more than just your home loan. People with bad credit likely have high interest rates on their car loans and their credit cards; even their auto insurance premiums are higher. All these extra charges can add up to thousands of extra dollars in interest payments each month.

> ## Your Credit Score:
> Those three little numbers can have a six-digit impact on your life.

Your credit score is your financial reputation. More than just a three-digit number, it is your key to the best house money can buy or the reason you might have suffered years of sleepless nights.

If you have bad credit, you will have problems finding an apartment to rent, much less a home to buy. Some employers won't consider hiring you because of your credit score. You will search frantically for a car loan, only to be disheartened by large monthly payments due to sky-high interest rates. Even your existing insurance premiums will be higher. Saving for your child's college tuition? A nice vacation? Forget about it— you can't afford them. And if you decide to take a vacation anyway, you will likely charge it to your high-interest credit card, further adding to your financial hardships.

This risky spending and subsequent compound interest can quickly spiral downward; you might miss a payment or two. Before you know it you are being hounded at home and at the office by aggressive collection agencies demanding payment on your delinquent financial accounts. Overwhelming, isn't it? Complicating matters, now you have to deal with the embarrassment of creditors calling your house all day. You just can't figure out how to dig yourself out of debt.

On the other hand, if your credit is good, lenders will compete for your business. You will qualify for the best loans on cars, homes, boats, furniture, or whatever you might choose to buy. Throughout the course of your life, you will save hundreds of thousands of dollars in interest, money you can apply to retirement savings, your child's college tuition, or investments. Countless offers for credit cards with low interest rates will flood your mailbox. You will have a padded bank account that allows you to buy vacation homes, start businesses, or retire early. Moreover, you will have peace of mind.

At least four out of every 10 people are paying higher mortgages than they would pay if they took a few simple steps to increase their credit, and about half have scores of less than 720. Shockingly, almost 80 percent have errors on their credit reports. And 25 percent have errors serious enough to cause the consumers to be turned down for loans or jobs.[1]

Clearly, most people have a lot of room for improvement but do not know what steps they need to take. They figure if they pay their bills on time each month they will have perfect credit. This is simply not true.

7 STEPS TO A 720 CREDIT SCORE is intended to provide step-by-step guidance on improving your credit score and avoiding the mistakes most consumers make. This book will help you leave the "bad credit cycle" and enter the "improving credit cycle." If you already have solid credit, you will find useful tips on maintaining and even enhancing your score.

Do you know that even if you pay your credit card balance in full each month, your credit might be harmed by a limit that is not as high as it should be?

Do you know that you should have no more than a 30 percent balance on each revolving credit account?

Do you know that using a credit card with no preset limit might hurt your credit score?

Do you know about the one type of credit that will always hurt your score?

---

1. 2004 U.S. Public Interest Research Group Survey.

7 STEPS TO A 720 CREDIT SCORE is a system for teaching you to play the credit game. Consider your credit score a little like an American playing European rugby. If you do not know the rules, you will fail, sometimes painfully! However, with a little guidance you can become a master of your credit score.

This book will prepare you for large purchases, such as homes or investment properties. By following the steps outlined, you will develop deep roots as a borrower. The deeper your roots, the less harmful a small blemish on your credit report will be.

Ours is not necessarily a quick fix, though I have seen people's credit score jump 50, even 100 points, in 30 days by following the **7 STEPS TO A 720 CREDIT SCORE**. More often, the **7 STEPS** is a time-tested system for improving and maintaining credit throughout your life. Unlike so-called "credit repair" books, **7 STEPS** does not encourage you to waste your valuable time trying to remove all past slip-ups from your credit report. Instead, it takes an alternative, more effective approach: this book will teach you to shift your behavior, leave your past mistakes behind, and start preparing your credit score for the future so that it will be a reliable asset for the rest of your life. The fundamental difference between **7 STEPS TO A 720 CREDIT SCORE** and other books on the market is that this book teaches the seven basic rules that, when applied, will result in a natural improvement of your credit score. Rather than asking you to focus on the past, the **7 STEPS** plan shows you how to modify your behavior and develop habits that will protect your credit score for a lifetime.

7 STEPS targets all levels of credit scores. If you have "subprime" credit (less than a 620 score), you will learn to alter your behavior to rebuild your credit. In two or three years (or sometimes immediately!), you'll see drastic improvements, allowing you to purchase a home at a lower interest rate. If you have average credit, you will learn a few tricks that are sure to push you to the next level so that you qualify for the lowest available interest rates. And if you have excellent credit, a 720 or better, you will find valuable knowledge that allows you to maintain your credit score during the ups and downs of life.

JIM

Jim, an optimistic college student majoring in English, received his first credit card when he was 18. He did not apply for the card; it just arrived in the mail. Jim took all his friends to dinner that night and bought his girlfriend an expensive necklace. From then on, his spending habits were out of control. He treated his friends to drinks, vacations, groceries, and whatever else fit on his credit card. Each month, he made the minimum $20 payment until his credit card balance reached its limit. Another arrived in the mail the following month, and the pattern repeated itself. By the time Jim was out of college, all five of his credit cards were over the limit, which meant that he was paying compound interest as well as a hefty "over-the-limit fee" each month.

Jim is now 25. Most of his credit card accounts have been turned over to collection agencies. With his modest salary as an English teacher, Jim is able to pay the collection companies a small monthly payment, but he has not been able to dig himself out of debt. In fact, his debt keeps growing. He has a high interest rate on his car and home loan, so he pays an extra $750 a month in interest. This is money he could put in savings or add toward paying off his debt. The added burden causes another problem: he keeps making late payments, lowering his credit score month after month. If Jim had read **7 STEPS TO A 720 CREDIT SCORE,** *he would know that he could improve his credit and refinance his mortgage if he stopped paying the collection companies and developed a structured debt-minimizing plan.*

CHARISS

A statistician, Chariss' job consists of analyzing numbers and determining risk. In October, she decides to finance a new television. Chariss shops for the best deal and finally settles on a store that promises: "Buy now, pay nothing until March of next year!" The sales representative assures her that she won't pay interest either. Chariss quickly does the math. For five months, she not only can save her monthly payment but also earn interest. When March arrives, she can make a large payment, which means her future interest payments will be less. Chariss is proud of herself. She's saving money, right? What Chariss doesn't know is that she's actually hurting her credit score, which means she'll pay higher interest rates on future loans.

BREEANNA

Breeanna, an accountant, has always been frugal. Her father, who went bankrupt when he was a young man, taught Breeanna to pay for everything with cash. She keeps a budget and tracks her spending to the penny. She rents a conservative apartment and drives an old car, which she bought with cash. She has just one credit card, which she uses only for emergencies. A very cautious person, Breeanna rarely has any emergencies. When she uses her credit card, she pays the bill in full the minute it arrives. Breeanna has plenty of money in savings.

*When Breeanna decides to buy a home, she figures it will be a simple process. She has always been a responsible spender. Why **wouldn't** a bank want to lend her money?*

When Breeanna came to me for a home loan, she was shocked to learn that her credit score was only 530, a whopping 190 points below the minimum credit score needed to qualify for the best interest rates. I explained that having very little credit is the same as having bad credit and that her conservative attitude toward debt had given the credit bureaus almost no information about her spending and paying habits. I gave Breeanna a copy of 7 STEPS TO A 720 CREDIT SCORE, *and we discussed the steps she needed to take: open more credit accounts, buy a car through an installment loan, and use her credit cards regularly.*

ROBERTO

Roberto's soon-to-be ex-wife maxed out their joint accounts, which are popping up on his credit report, along with all the payments she failed to make on time. Roberto constantly has to pay her bills to keep them from being sent to collection agencies and further damaging his credit. This means he makes late payments from time to time on his own bills. He thinks he will just have to weather the storm and then wait seven years before his credit is repaired.

Looking to buy a house, Roberto accepts that he will have a high interest rate. He does not realize that with a few simple steps (such as canceling joint credit cards), Roberto could easily improve his credit and qualify for the best loan available.

KERRY

Kerry is ready to buy his first home. He researches the market and keeps his credit fairly clean. When he applies for a loan through another lender, he finds he has a 717 credit score. His mortgage broker tells him that if he raises his credit score by three points, he will qualify for a much better loan. Kerry pays off a credit card and closes the account. Even though it was just a year away from dropping off his credit report, Kerry pays a six-year-old bill in collection, assuming that by paying the collection account, his score will jump immediately. When Kerry reapplies for the loan, he is surprised to find that his score had dropped. What happened? Why did Kerry's credit score fall so much and so quickly?

Answers to these questions were once a mystery. We could speculate, but no one really knew how credit scores were calculated. Credit bureaus considered this information a closely guarded secret. They figured if consumers knew how credit scores were assigned, they would come up with strategies to improve their scores. If this happened, scoring firms worried that the formulas they used would lose their ability to accurately predict spending behavior. Fortunately, due to increasing pressure from Congress and consumer groups, scoring firms finally released the 22 criteria used to determine credit scores. This book summarizes these criteria and gives instructions on maximizing your credit potential. It also dispels myths that popped up years ago as lenders and credit experts tried to guess how the formulas were determined.

What this book does **not** provide are the exact formulas used to determine credit scores. These formulas have not been released, and they probably never will be. Though we do know the variables (all 22 of them), we do not always know how they affect each other, nor do we know when the formulas are modified to reflect changes in consumer spending habits.

Although this book is an excellent tool, it is not an exact science. We feel confident that all of these steps will help your credit score in the long run; **however, some of the information might initially hurt your score** (it's the "one step back, two steps forward" concept). If you plan on making a large purchase in the next few months, your credit cannot afford a setback. Rather, consult with a mortgage broker or credit specialist who will take a personalized approach toward improving your credit score. This is particularly important if you plan on buying a home or investment property within the next 12 months. Some credit specialists and mortgage brokers (including me) have tools that allow us to make updates to your credit score within 24 hours. If you try the same thing on your own, it might take 30, 60, sometimes 120 days for your credit score to reflect the change. This could mean the difference between 10, 20, or even 100 points, which translates into thousands of dollars in interest. For a referral to a mortgage broker or credit improvement specialist, call **(877) 720-SCORE**.

Using the 7 Steps to
Apply for a Home Loan

This book allows you to take a wealth of knowledge to the table when applying for a home loan, but the book alone is not enough if your score is less than 720. To maximize your credit and minimize your mortgage payments, you will also need a mortgage broker who will work with you to increase your credit score and lower your interest rate. Many mortgage brokers look at your credit and give you a loan based on your current score. Rather, you want a mortgage broker who will look at the best available loan and help you increase your credit to qualify for that loan.

For instance, a client came to me after failing to get a loan through several lenders. I studied his credit report and noticed a collection notice from a debt his deceased wife had not paid. Because he had been an authorized user on his wife's account, his score had been damaged as well.

We contacted the creditor, explained the situation, and removed his name from the account. By doing this, his score increased 59 points. He now qualifies for the loans he wasn't previously able to obtain.

Your mortgage broker should take the same approach. When you apply for a loan, your mortgage broker should tell you what your payments will look like if you increase your credit score by 5, 10, 30, or even 100 points.

Armed with the 7 STEPS, you can develop a plan to reach your goal. You might not have to hire or pay anyone. In fact, you should be aware that some credit repair companies are ineffective; they suppress rather than delete derogatory items, meaning the items will come back to haunt you later. Others provide the same services that you, using the 7 STEPS, can easily manage on your own.

If you need help implementing these steps, you might want to find a trustworthy credit improvement specialist nonetheless. For a referral to a credit improvement specialist, lender, or any other industry professional, visit our website at **WWW.7STEPSTO720.COM,** or call **(877) 720-SCORE.**

One Final Note
Before We Jump In

Poor credit can be embarrassing. Like many people with credit difficulties, you might have ignored your financial problems, which has probably made them worse. You might think that your poor financial record is a sign of poor character. But I can tell you that this is not true. Bad credit happens to all types of people (Walt Disney and Mark Twain both claimed bankruptcy). Bad credit can slowly creep up on you. It might occur because of a crisis, a job loss, a divorce, or a sudden illness.

And yes, let's not forget, sometimes it happens because you made irresponsible and rash decisions or because you mismanaged your money.

But that was in the past. You are not making bad or uneducated decisions now. You are making a decision to improve your credit and deal with it head on by developing a solid plan of attack. That makes you a responsible person, and it demonstrates good character.

Now let's move forward so we can put your bad credit in the past.

KEY POINTS

CREDIT AND THE AMERICAN DREAM

7 STEPS TO A 720 CREDIT SCORE provides both history about credit scoring and advice on improving your credit score. Though both of these aspects of the credit industry are important, the latter is crucial. If you don't have time to read this entire book, flip ahead to the **KEY POINTS** section at the end of each chapter, where you will find a synopsis of the steps you should take to improve your credit.

credit facts

Your credit score is a three-digit rating that generally ranges from 300 to 850. The score is based on constantly changing mathematical formulas used by lenders to predict whether a borrower will pay debt on time and in full. The credit scoring system is designed to give creditors a concrete answer to the following question: "What is the likelihood that this borrower will be more than 90 days late within the next 24 months?"

A borrower with an 850 score is considered low risk, the least likely to default on payments, while a borrower with a 300 score is considered high risk, the most likely to default. In general, lenders provide the best interest rates for borrowers with credit scores of 720 or higher. Borrowers with scores below 620 are considered "subprime" borrowers. Considered high risk, these borrowers are given higher interest rates.

If you have a credit score of...	Then...
720 or above	You have wonderful credit and will qualify for loans and interest rates reserved for borrowers in the highest echelon.
700 - 719	You have excellent credit and are considered low risk, but you might not qualify for the best loans and your interest rates might drop if you raised your score a few extra points.
660 - 699	You have fair to good credit. You might qualify for a strong loan but only if the rest of your application is strong. You definitely won't receive the best loans or the lowest interest rates.
620 - 659	You have weak to borderline credit. The rest of your file will need to be perfect to qualify for an acceptable loan. You will pay higher interest rates and your loan terms will be less than ideal.
Below 620	You have poor credit. Your loan terms will be far from ideal. You pay the highest interest rates. The lower your score, the worse your terms.

According to Fair Isaac Company (FICO), about 50 percent of people have credit scores that fall below 720, while 20 percent fall below 620.

Your credit score is perhaps the most important factor in determining whether lenders approve your credit card application, mortgage loan, or car loan. **It matters more than your annual salary and much, much more than your net worth.** Once you have a 720 credit score, lenders will start competing for your business, and you will be offered the best interest rates available.

In January 2005, a borrower with a 720 or higher credit score would likely pay $1,730 per month (at 5.64 percent interest) on a $300,000, 30-year fixed-rate mortgage. As you can see in the following table, the numbers change drastically if the person's score is less than 720. At scores under 620, a borrower would pay $2,319 a month, $589 more than the borrower with a 720 credit score!

ESTIMATED INTEREST RATES AND CORRESPONDING PAYMENTS

Score	Interest	Payment
720 - 850	5.64%	$1,730
700 - 719	5.77%	$1,754
675 - 699	6.30%	$1,858
620 - 674	7.45%	$2,088
560 - 619	8.53%	$2,319
500 - 559	9.29%	$2,476

Rates determined by FICO (www.myfico.com) on January 23, 2005.
Rates updated daily. Actual payments determined by loan type and current interest rates.

Who Reports Your Credit Score?

As I've alluded to, the credit-scoring world is a complicated one that is further complicated by all of the players involved. In fact, your credit score will be different depending on who is asking for your score and who is reporting your score.

Confused? Let's start with how it changes based on who is making the request.

If a mortgage broker asks for your score, he will see a very different number than if you ask for your score. This is because the primary credit reporting bureaus (Equifax, TransUnion, and Experian) tailor the formula according to the person/company "pulling" the credit report. An automobile company is more interested than a landlord in your payment history as it relates to installment loans. As such, the different credit bureaus apply four different formulas depending on who is asking for your credit report:

- ❖ The **consumer formula** is used if you request your own score.
- ❖ The **auto formula** is the formula the credit bureaus use for lenders considering whether to give you an installment loan.
- ❖ The **tenant screening formula** is used for landlords considering whether to rent to you.
- ❖ The **FICO formula** is used for mortgage brokers and other creditors (e.g., Visa®, MasterCard®, etc.) considering whether to extend a home loan, credit card, or line of credit. The FICO score is the most common score provided to creditors.

For this reason, if you purchase your own credit score online, it will not be the same score seen by lenders. Instead, you will see your consumer score, which will most likely be drastically different from the score seen by creditors and landlords. I tested this with my own credit score and found a 31-point difference between my consumer score and my FICO score on the same day.

Weaving a more intricate web, let's introduce some additional players. As I mentioned, your score changes based on who is reporting it. The three major credit bureaus (TransUnion, Equifax, and Experian) are responsible for monitoring credit activity and reporting credit scores. However, not all creditors provide information to each credit bureau, which means that each bureau generally will report a different score. So how do lenders determine your credit score? When determining your interest rate for any given loan or credit card, they look at your middle score and assign that rating to you. For instance, if Experian gives you a 721 credit rating, TransUnion gives you a 680, and Equifax a 612, lenders will consider 680 your credit score.

If this is confusing, don't worry. Just remember two important things: 1) your credit report will show a different number if you pull it yourself; and 2) though this book focuses on FICO scores (the score used by lenders when determining the terms and rate of your home loan or credit card), all of the information included in this book will help boost your score, regardless of the formula used.

Fair Isaac Company (FICO) was founded in 1956 by Bill Fair, an engineer, and Earl Isaac, a mathematician. Together, the two created the FICO scoring system, a mathematical formula used to predict the likelihood of a borrower paying bills on time and in full. FICO is the standard credit scoring system used by the primary three credit bureaus—Equifax, TransUnion, and Experian—to report a borrower's credit score to mortgage brokers and creditors.

What Factors Determine
Your Credit Score?

Generally speaking, items stay on your credit report for seven years. Anytime you apply for credit, take out a loan, make a payment, or fail to make a payment, the activity is reported to the credit bureaus. Likewise, anytime you apply for a loan, credit card, or line of credit, the lender checks your credit score to determine your risk level. As a result, your credit score can change from day-to-day, even hour-to-hour. New information is reported to your account, old information is deleted, and your score adjusts accordingly. A good score can become a bad score in the blink of an eye. Sadly, it is much more difficult to turn a bad score into a good score; points are difficult to gain and easy to lose.

Though your credit score is based on approximately 22 different criteria, **five factors make up the bulk of the formula**, as shown in the following figure: 1) your payment history; 2) the amount of money you owe; 3) the length of time you have had credit; 4) the type of credit you have; and 5) credit inquiries.

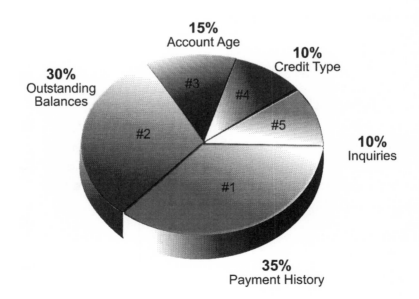

YOUR PAYMENT HISTORY

Your payment history accounts for approximately 35 percent of your credit score, making it the single-most important part of your score. This component considers the frequency of your late payments, the severity of the derogatory payments, and the recency of late payments. It includes:

❖ Your payment history on mortgages, installment loans (e.g., car loans), revolving accounts (e.g., credit cards), student loans, and retail accounts (e.g., Macy's® card).

❖ The details of your late payments, including how frequently and how recently you have been late on payments. Late payments incurred within six months have the greatest impact on your credit score, while late payments more than 24 months old have very little impact on your credit score. Having one or two late payments is not necessarily going to ruin your score. An overall solid credit history is more important than one or two blemishes.

❖ Repossessions, collection, charge-offs, and public records (e.g., bankruptcies or foreclosures). These are among the most harmful activities on your credit report, and most stay on for seven years, though bankruptcies stay for 10 years. Older items and delinquencies on accounts with small balances will damage your score less than recent items or accounts with large balances.

❖ The number of accounts with no late payments.

Your payment history is weighed on a scale with the most recent payment activity given more weight than past activity. Recent late payments affect your score more severely than aging ones. The credit scoring models assume that your current performance is a far better indicator of your credit-worthiness than your past behavior. Your current behavior, after all, can better forecast whether you are experiencing a downward financial turn. For this reason, if you make a late payment on an otherwise spotless credit report, your credit score will probably drop more than if you have been consistently late. This is because a negative change in normal behavior is considered a warning sign of a shift in your financial situation. If making late payments is your standard, the credit scoring industry assumes your financial situation is stable and that you will probably make the payment eventually. You will be docked points each time you make a late payment, but the decline will be much more gradual.

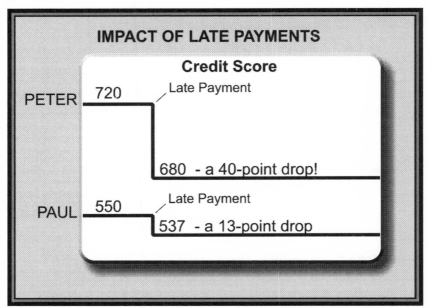

THE AMOUNT OF MONEY YOU OWE

The amount of money you owe, or your outstanding debt, makes up 30 percent of your credit score, which is based on your "utilization rate," the debt you carry as a percentage of your limit. Revolving accounts with a balance of 30 percent or less of the total credit limit provide better scores than accounts that exceed the 30 percent threshold. As a result, borrowers who transfer all of their debt onto one credit card with the lowest interest rate might be helping their immediate finances, but they are likely hurting their credit score, which will hurt their finances in the long run. You are better off spreading your debt among three credit cards, each with a 30 percent (or less) utilization rate. (Note that your score is **not** affected by a utilization rate that is "too low." Some consumers mistakenly believe that their credit scores will drop if they have "too much" available credit.)

Having a high utilization rate on credit cards tells lenders that you might be overextended and are more likely to make late payments.

This criterion also measures your loans (e.g., auto or home) by comparing how much you owe against how much you originally borrowed. If you have a new home loan, credit bureaus generally see you as more of a risk than someone with a five- or 10-year-old loan with consistent on-time payments.

THE LENGTH OF TIME YOU HAVE HAD CREDIT

The length of time you have had credit affects about 15 percent of your score. The longer an account has been open, the better the score. This component looks at both active accounts and inactive accounts. If you have a credit card that was opened in 1970 and closed in 1990, the account should still be on your credit report and its age (20 years) factored into your credit score. This component also considers the average age of your accounts, which means that each time you open a new account, the average age is lowered, and your credit score is lowered accordingly. For instance, if you have two accounts that have each been open for seven years, the average age of your accounts is seven years. If you open a third account, the average age will drop to 4.7 years.

1. Capital One	84 months old (7 years)
	+
2. Citibank Preferred	84 months old (7 years)
Average Age: 84 months (7 years)	
vs.	
1. Capital One	84 months old (7 years)
	+
2. Citibank Preferred	84 months old (7 years)
	+
3. Bravo	**1 month old**
Average Age: 56.3 months (4.7 years)	

Finally, remember that credit scoring systems deduct points initially when you open new credit accounts; they award points once you have made a few timely payments and proven that the new loan is something you can manage.

THE TYPE OF CREDIT YOU HAVE

The type of credit you have accounts for 10 percent of your score. Credit bureaus want to see a healthy mix of credit, especially if you have a limited credit history. Ideally, you should have a mortgage, an installment loan (e.g., car, boat, or furniture loan), and at least three major revolving accounts (i.e., Visa®, MasterCard®, American Express®, and Discover®).

Contrary to common belief, having too little credit can hurt your score. If you do not have any credit cards, home loans, or installment loans, you probably have a lower score than someone who has managed credit responsibly. You might even have a lower score than someone with a poor credit history. The credit scoring models want to see that you have the discipline to manage debt and high limits.

That said, one type of credit will always hurt your score. For the purpose of this book, we'll call these "finance accounts" or "finance cards." Finance accounts, which appear on your credit report as installment loans, are those that allow you to delay payments for more than 30 days after purchasing an item. Alternatively, they might allow you to defer interest, or pay interest only, for a specific period of time. If you purchase a television in June and are told that you do not need to make payments until January of the following year, you are hurting your credit with a finance account.

Finance accounts usually are offered in furniture, electronic, or appliance stores and can be tricky to spot. For one thing, some stores offer both retail accounts and finance accounts. Retail accounts are store-specific accounts that require payment within 30 days of first use and are treated as revolving accounts; they do not hurt your score so long as you make regular payments and keep your balance low. Finance accounts, the harmful credit accounts, delay payments for more than 30 days.

Some retail accounts have billing cycles that are longer than 30 days but are not considered finance accounts—these are not delaying payments, but rather lengthening the billing cycle. As I said, finance accounts can be tricky to spot. If you are ever in a store applying for a line of credit, ask the store representative if you can speak directly with the finance representative prior to entering into the loan. Be aware that the store representative probably hasn't read **7 STEPS TO A 720 CREDIT SCORE** and, therefore, probably knows little to nothing about the type of credit you are considering. Speak with the finance representative directly or refuse the account.

Finance accounts are the only type of credit account that will hurt your score every time. For this reason, apply for them sparingly and be strategic. If you are planning on making a large purchase within the next few months and you have borderline credit, don't apply for a finance account.

CREDIT INQUIRIES

Credit inquiries account for approximately 10 percent of your credit score. As you already know, opening accounts will damage your score initially. Likewise, inquiries (i.e., potential lenders requesting your credit score) will hurt your credit score. The credit bureaus see this as potentially risky, figuring you might be preparing to go on a credit card spending spree. Having too many inquiries is especially harmful if your credit is relatively young.

Many consumers are more concerned about credit inquiries than they need be. For instance, you might be surprised to hear that your score will not be harmed by inquiries into your own credit report. If you request your own score, the inquiry will show up on your credit report as a "soft" inquiry. Unlike "hard" inquiries (those pulled by lenders), soft inquiries do not affect your credit score.

Credit bureaus make exceptions for people who are shopping around for the best home loan or car loan, counting all loan officer inquiries within a 45-day period as just one inquiry.

Credit inquiries affect your score for only one year, although they stay on your credit report for two years.

THE 22 CRITERIA THAT DETERMINE A CREDIT SCORE[1]

FICO uses 22 criteria to design an intricate formula used to determine your credit score. These criteria include:

1) Account payment information on credit cards, retail accounts, installment loans, finance accounts, mortgages, and other credit accounts

2) Presence of or lack of adverse public records, such as bankruptcies, judgments, suits, liens, wage attachments, as well as collection items, and delinquencies

3) Duration an account is past due (items 90 days past due are more severe than those 30 days past due)

4) Amount past due

5) Recency of past due items, public records, or collection items

6) Number of delinquent items on your credit report

7) Number of accounts on your credit report that are in good standing (e.g., "paid as agreed")

8) Amount you owe on all accounts

9) Amount you owe on individual accounts

10) Type of balance you carry (or do not carry)

11) Number of accounts that have balances

12) Utilization rate on revolving accounts

13) Proportion of your balance as it relates to the original amount of your installment loans

14) Average time since accounts were opened

15) Time since each account was opened

16) Time since the last account activity

17) Number of recently opened accounts, as well as the proportion of accounts that are recently opened

18) Number of credit inquiries

19) Time since the most recent accounts were opened

20) Time since the credit inquiries

21) Following past payment problems, the re-establishment of positive credit

22) The mix of various types of credit

1. As reported online at **WWW.MYFICO.COM/CREDITEDUCATION/WHATSINYOURSCORE.ASPX**.

CRITERIA THAT DO NOT AFFECT YOUR CREDIT SCORE

1) Education level

2) The number of years you have lived in a single location

3) Surprisingly, your salary

4) "Late" payments that occur less than 30 days past the due date (or, in some cases, less than one billing cycle past the due date). It's true that paying a bill late is perhaps the most common way to damage your credit score. What you might not know is that the bureaus do not consider a payment late until it is 30 days or more past the due date. For instance, if your American Express® bill is to be paid by January 1, credit bureaus do not consider it late until January 31. (Note that credit card companies still charge a late fee if you make a payment even one day past the due date.)

5) Late payments on utility bills, such as gas, electric, phone, cable, or cell phone. (However, if these payments are turned over to a collection agency, your credit will be damaged.)

6) Bounced checks, unless the debt is turned over to a collection company

7) Rent payment history, unless you are evicted

8) Child support or alimony obligations, so long as you pay on time

9) Race, religion, nationality, gender, or marital status

10) Age

11) Occupation or employment history

12) Interest charged on a credit card

13) Inquiries you make into your credit report and inquiries made by employers

People with little or no credit history might be saddened to learn that the bureaus usually do not look at timely rent or utility payments when calculating your credit score. However, if you are buying a house, lenders will want to see verification of timely rent payment. A new system, the FICO Expansion Score, does look at these activities, allowing credit bureaus to better evaluate people with little or no credit history. However, if you fall into this category, you probably should not rely on the FICO Expansion Score, as it is still relatively new and rarely used.

How Much and for How Long Do Activities Affect Your Credit?

By now, you know that most items fall off a credit report after seven years, bankruptcies stay for 10 years, and credit inquiries fall off a report in two years. Liens (claims made by a creditor against a borrower's property as security for money owed) stay on your report for seven years from the time they are satisfied (i.e., from the time they are paid in full).

But having an item on your credit report and having it affect your credit score are two different things. Most lenders look only at your credit score, though a few look at your credit report to see the details behind the number.

The affect of one activity on your overall credit score is difficult to tell without the formula and all related variables. **7 STEPS TO A 720 CREDIT SCORE** will give you an idea of how certain activities affect your credit score.

Keep in mind, this is an educated guess based on my experience reviewing thousands of credit reports. Your credit report might behave differently depending on the specifics of your credit history. As well, credit scoring models are constantly changing, so you should check with a credit specialist for the most updated information specific to your unique credit report.

Where Can You Find Your Credit Report and Score?

By now you know that pulling your own credit report does not hurt your score. You are probably thinking, *I should pull my credit report often!* You are right. If you live in the United States, you should request a copy of your credit report from each of the three major bureaus, which can be contacted by phone or online as shown below:

Equifax
(800) 685-1111
WWW.EQUIFAX.COM

Experian
(888) 397-3742
WWW.EXPERIAN.COM

TransUnion
(800) 888-4213
WWW.TRANSUNION.COM

Unless you have been denied credit (in which case you can request a free copy of your credit report from all three bureaus), you will have to pay for your credit report, though once a year you can receive a free copy of each credit report from **WWW.ANNUALCREDITREPORT.COM**. Note that your credit report and your credit score are not the same thing. Don't bother purchasing your credit score—the score you receive will be your consumer score, not your FICO score. It will be drastically different than the score lenders will see when they pull your report.

If you want to know what your credit score is, call a lender and ask her to pull your report and credit score. This will give you a more accurate picture of your current position. Call **(877) 720-SCORE** for a referral to a lender.

Regardless of where you obtain it, your credit report is a useful tool in that you can monitor the activity on the report and make sure there are no errors. You should request a copy of your credit report regularly—at least once every six months. If you are trying to increase your score, you might want to request your credit report more often. This will allow you to monitor activities and catch any negative information added to your credit report.

Credit Myths

Before credit bureaus released the variables they used to assign credit scores, mortgage brokers, lenders, and credit experts took some educated guesses on which factors determined a person's score. As it turned out, they were right most of the time, but not always. As a result, many borrowers are operating under credit myths.

MYTH #1:
The less credit I have, the better my score will be.

Fact: As much sense as this might make to you, it is not true, regardless of what your grandfather says. Credit bureaus want to see that you can handle credit responsibly. Consumers who declare bankruptcy often wipe their hands clean of debt, saying they will never again have another credit card. But what they might not realize is that no credit is just as bad as poor credit. The best way to have a solid credit score is to have a healthy mix of credit and a solid payment history. You have to prove to the bureaus you have the discipline to handle credit. The only way to do this is to have a proven track record.

MYTH #2:
I can raise my credit score by asking my credit card companies to lower my limits.

Fact: This goes along with **MYTH #1**, and it is usually untrue. If you lower your limit without lowering your balance, your utilization rate will be too high, and credit bureaus see this as dangerous.

MYTH #3:
If I close some of my credit card accounts, I will have a better score.

Fact: Credit experts generally agree that once you have opened accounts you should keep them open. Closing them will never help your score, and it might actually hurt your score by lowering your overall utilization rate and shortening the average age of your active accounts.

MYTH #4:
I have to keep a balance to have a good credit score.

Fact: Sadly, this mistaken belief causes some consumers to make unnecessary interest payments. The truth of the matter is credit bureaus have no way of knowing whether you pay your balance in full each month or whether you make monthly payments. If you have the financial resources to do so, pay off your balance each month! It can't hurt your score; in fact, it might help your score by lowering your utilization rate. I should note that I have heard of cases where a small balance and recent activity on a credit card have boosted a person's score enough to give him a better interest rate on a loan. That said, the increase is minimal. Generally speaking, keeping a balance is unnecessary, though it won't hurt (and might help) to have a small balance when your credit report is pulled for a loan.

MYTH #5:
If I request my credit report, I will hurt my credit score.

Fact: It is true that having too many inquiries **by lenders** hurts your credit report, but how frequently you pull **your own** credit report has no negative impact on your score. The inquiry will show up on your credit report but will not affect your score. Credit bureaus know you need to monitor your credit report, so pulling your own report is considered responsible behavior. Do it freely! Remember that you shouldn't bother paying for your credit score because it will be the consumer score and not the FICO score used by lenders.

MYTH #6:
I cannot get credit because I have had a bankruptcy, a foreclosure, a tax lien, or a bill turned over for collection.

Fact: Although it is true that you will likely pay higher interest rates, certain lenders market to people with problem credit. However, getting a lot of credit might not be wise if you are having financial difficulties. Moreover, you probably can't afford the high interest rates. But, having a small amount of credit will help rebuild your score. If you have poor credit, you can, and should, apply for a credit card immediately. You need to start rebuilding your credit now.

MYTH #7:
Consumer credit counseling will hurt my credit score.

Fact: If you are using consumer credit counseling, credit bureaus will list this on your credit report but will not use this information to calculate your score (though they did in the past). Regardless, consumer credit counseling can indirectly hurt your credit score. Consumer credit counseling companies are hired to handle your accounts. This means that creditors will not notify you about the status of your account; they will notify the consumer credit counseling service. It works like this: you pay the service a chunk of money each month. In turn, the consumer credit counseling service disperses the money as it sees fit. It might, or might not, be making your minimum payments. Most of the time, the service will miss payments, but you might not know this because the creditor will communicate directly with the consumer credit counseling service.

If a consumer credit counselor does not pay your bills on time, guess what? Your credit score suffers. For this reason, you should be wary of some consumer counselors.

And there is more than one reason to avoid consumer credit counseling: some lenders will not approve loans for people with consumer counseling, regardless of how good their credit score is.

MYTH #8:
If I pay my bills on time and in full each month, I'll have perfect credit.

Fact: This is perhaps the most pervasive myth, but it isn't true. As you have already learned, a lot of other criteria affect your credit score. Keep reading for a full picture.

MYTH #9:
I can increase my credit score by paying my collection accounts.

Fact: You will most likely hurt your credit score by paying accounts in collection. We will discuss this in depth in **STEP 6,** but for now you should know that paying a debt in collection not only will damage your score further but also will extend the amount of time a negative item stays on your credit report. To guard against this, you should consider refusing to pay the account until the creditor or collection agency agrees to wipe the derogatory activity off your credit report.

MYTH #10:
I can get my credit score for free online.

Fact: You will always have to pay for your credit score (unless it is pulled by a lender). Some companies will provide your credit report for free, but they will not include your credit score. To view your credit score, you will need to pay a fee (usually about $13 per credit score). Also note that not all credit scores are equal. Different companies use different methods of collecting data. For instance, automobile companies are interested in the specifics of your credit history as they pertain to installment loans. Most companies that offer credit scores to consumers (e.g., **WWW.ANNUALCREDITREPORT.COM**) use a different system than the one used by mortgage brokers and credit card companies, who use the FICO system. If you purchase your credit score online, it will likely be quite different than the credit score your mortgage broker or lender will have. For this reason, you should ask a mortgage broker or lender to pull your credit report. Call **(877) 720-SCORE** for a referral.

MYTH #11:

I will hurt my credit if I change lenders.

Fact: This is a myth that unscrupulous mortgage brokers perpetuate to secure your business. If your lender tells you that your credit will be damaged if you switch lenders, he is not telling the truth. Though the new lender will want to pull your credit report, credit bureaus treat all inquiries from a mortgage broker that occur within 45 days as one inquiry. If you don't like your lender, choose another one quickly.

Is Credit the Only Thing Lenders Consider?

It depends. When buying a home, lenders usually consider your credit score, your down payment, your income, and the amount of savings you have. If your credit score is high enough (above a 720), many lenders will place less weight (if any) on other factors. Credit scores that fall below 620, classified as "subprime," result in high interest rates, regardless of your income, savings, or down payment (though these factors will matter more in determining your interest rate than they would if you had credit above a 720). A majority of lenders will ignore 70 percent of an application if a person's credit is pristine.

The 7 Steps

Now that you have learned the basics, it is time to learn the **7 STEPS**. The rest of this book, as well as the accompanying workbook (**APPLYING THE 7 STEPS TO A 720 CREDIT SCORE WORKBOOK**), which you can purchase online at **WWW.7STEPSTO720.COM**, will go into greater detail, help you apply the **7 STEPS**, and provide forms and worksheets to help you accomplish your goal of a 720 credit score.

THE 7 STEPS TO A 720 CREDIT SCORE:

STEP 1: Keep your credit card balances under 30 percent of your credit limit.

STEP 2: Have at least three revolving credit lines.

STEP 3: Verify the accuracy of your reported credit limits.

STEP 4: Have at least one helpful active or paid installment loan on your credit report.

STEP 5: Remove high-priority errors from your credit report.

STEP 6: Negotiate for a letter of deletion before paying a bill in collection.

STEP 7: Create a structured plan to protect your credit.

Read on. You are about to change your financial future.

KEY POINTS

CREDIT FACTS

Credit is the most important factor lenders consider when deciding whether you are qualified for a loan. Credit is determined primarily by five factors:

YOUR PAYMENT HISTORY. This includes the history on your accounts, both positive and negative, as well as any collections, repossessions, bankruptcies, or foreclosures you might have. More recent activities have a greater impact on your score than older activities.

THE AMOUNT OF MONEY YOU OWE. This score is based on your "utilization rate," the debt you carry as a percentage of your limit. Revolving accounts with a balance of 30 percent or less of the total credit limit provide better scores than accounts that exceed the 30 percent threshold.

THE LENGTH OF TIME YOU HAVE HAD CREDIT. The older your accounts, the better. You shouldn't close old accounts, and you should be strategic about opening new accounts.

THE TYPE OF CREDIT YOU HAVE. Credit bureaus want to see a healthy mix of credit on your report. They will respond best if you have a mortgage loan, an installment loan, and three revolving accounts.

CREDIT INQUIRIES. Too many inquiries (i.e., potential lenders requesting your credit score) in a one-year period will hurt your credit score. Credit scoring systems see this as potentially risky, figuring you might be preparing to go on a credit card spending spree. Having too many inquiries is especially harmful if your credit is relatively young. That said, many consumers are more concerned about credit inquiries than they need to be. For instance, you might be surprised to hear that your score will not be harmed by inquiries

KEY POINTS   continued

into your own credit report. If you request your own credit report, the inquiry will show up on your report as a "soft" inquiry. Unlike "hard" inquiries (those pulled by lenders), soft inquiries do not affect your credit score.

In general, lenders provide the best interest rates for borrowers with credit scores of 720 or higher. Borrowers with scores below 620 are considered "subprime" borrowers. Considered high risk, these borrowers receive the highest interest rates.

In fact, on a $300,000 home loan, the difference between a poor credit score (below 620) and a great credit score (720 or above) is about $589 a month. Over 30 years, that's $212,040!

To raise your score to 720 and above, follow the **7 STEPS** outlined in this book:

STEP 1:   Keep your credit card balances under 30 percent of your credit limit.

STEP 2:   Have at least three revolving credit lines.

STEP 3:   Verify the accuracy of your reported credit limits.

STEP 4:   Have at least one helpful active or paid installment loan on your credit report.

STEP 5:   Remove high-priority errors from your credit report.

STEP 6:   Negotiate for a letter of deletion before paying a bill in collection.

STEP 7:   Create a structured plan to protect your credit.

Remember: credit scoring models, as well as laws regulating the industry, are constantly changing. For up-to-date information about your unique credit report, call **(877) 720-SCORE** or visit **WWW.7STEPSTO720.COM** for more information, or for a referral to a credit specialist.

step**1**

Keep Your Credit Card Balances Under 30 Percent of Your Credit Limit

JACKSON

Jackson was a model citizen. He paid his bills on time, always drove under the speed limit, and never cheated on his taxes. He used less than half the credit available on most of his five credit cards and usually paid the balance in full at the end of each month. Sure, he had a couple of low-interest cards that were almost maxed out by the time the bill arrived, but Jackson had three others that he used only for emergencies.

When I told Jackson that he might be able to refinance and take advantage of lower interest rates, he didn't think twice. Of course he would refinance!

But he was shocked to learn that his credit score had dropped since he purchased his home five years previously. As a result, he was no longer eligible for the lowest interest rates. Jackson felt his credit should be better—after all, he had a mortgage loan on his account. He had never even missed a payment; so, what was the problem?

I analyzed his credit report and found that while Jackson's payment habits had not changed, his spending habits were markedly different since he purchased his home. Before, he never spent more than 30 percent of his credit cards' limits. The extra burden of the mortgage payment caused him to finance more of his expenses using his credit cards. In proportion to his credit limits, Jackson's balance was too high, and credit bureaus saw him as a risk.

To increase or maintain your credit score, your balance on any one credit card should never exceed 30 percent of your limit. For instance, if you have a $10,000 limit on your Visa® card, keep your total charges at no more than $3,000. The debt you carry on a credit card in proportion to your balance is called a "utilization rate," and credit scoring models respond more favorably if your utilization rate is low.

Credit Limit	Ideal Balance
$1,000	$300
$2,000	$600
$3,000	$900
$4,000	$1,200
$5,000	$1,500
$6,000	$1,800
$7,000	$2,100
$8,000	$2,400
$9,000	$2,700
$10,000	$3,000
$11,000	$3,300
$12,000	$3,600
$13,000	$3,900
$14,000	$4,200
$15,000	$4,500
$16,000	$4,800
$17,000	$5,100
$18,000	$5,400
$19,000	$5,700
$20,000	$6,000

Why the 30 percent rule? Lenders want a fair assessment of whether you will repay your debt. By showing responsible use of your credit cards, you fit the profile of someone more likely to repay debt. The higher your utilization rate, the more financially strained you appear to the credit bureaus. It makes sense: when people begin having financial problems, many turn to their credit cards to pay day-to-day living expenses. As their balance mounts, they incur higher utilization rates.

If you pay off your balance each month, you might assume it does not matter whether you exceed the 30 percent threshold. **Beware of this assumption**. Your credit report will show the balance on the day it is pulled. Consequently, be sure that you always keep no more than a 30 percent balance. A client of mine paid his bills on time and in full on the last day of each month. When we pulled his credit report on January 27, he was disappointed to see that his credit score had dropped.

We waited one week, pulled his credit report again, and his credit score had increased substantially. As a result, he was able to qualify for a great interest rate. But he learned his lesson: to keep his credit strong from day-to-day, my client now keeps his utilization rate less than 30 percent throughout the month. You should too, especially because some mortgage brokers do not understand the rules of the credit game. Their clients pay thousands of dollars extra each month simply because the lender pulled the credit report on the wrong day of the month.

You should also ensure that you have no more than a 30 percent balance on each credit card. An overall, combined 30 percent balance will not suffice.

Some consumers want to make all their charges on the credit card with the lowest interest rate. You might be surprised that I advise against this. After all, wouldn't you save money by making all your charges on your card with the lowest interest rate? The truth is this will save you money if you carry a balance, but only initially. In the long run, you will pay for utilizing this strategy, especially if you are planning on buying a home within the next six months. For example, if you are over the 30 percent utilization rate on your low-interest rate card, your credit score will be negatively affected and the interest rate on your home loan will be higher. Remember: higher credit scores translate into hundreds of thousands of dollars in interest payment savings.

What if You Have a Utilization Rate Above 30 Percent?

If your utilization rate exceeds 30 percent on a credit card, you have several options:

OPTION A: Transfer funds so that each card has a 30 percent balance or less; and/or

OPTION B: Pay off any debts that put your balance above 30 percent of the limit; and/or

OPTION C: Ask your credit card company to increase your limit so that your balance is less than 30 percent; and/or

OPTION D: Open another credit card account and transfer balances accordingly (but only after reading STEP 2).

OPTION A: TRANSFER FUNDS SO THAT EACH CARD HAS A 30 PERCENT BALANCE OR LESS

This option is probably the easiest but is not always available. Transferring funds works only if your other credit cards will incur less than a 30 percent utilization rate after the debt is transferred. If transferring funds causes another card to exceed 30 percent, then don't bother. Instead, choose another option.

EXAMPLE

You have three credit cards: a MasterCard®, Visa®, and Discover®. Your MasterCard® limit is $10,000 while your balance is $7,000. Your Visa® limit is $6,000, and your balance is $100. Your Discover® limit is $10,000 and your balance is $250.

The following table details the appropriate balance for each card, as well as the actual utilization rate.

Card	Credit Limit	Debt (Balance)	Appropriate (Balance)	Utilization Rate
MasterCard®	$10,000	$7,000	$\leq$ $3,000	70%
Visa®	$6,000	$100	$\leq$ $1,800	2%
Discover®	$10,000	$250	$\leq$ $3,000	2.5%

Even though your Visa® and Discover® cards are well below the 30 percent threshold, your credit is being harmed because of the high balance on your MasterCard®. You are $4,000 over the 30 percent limit. But there is an easy solution: luckily, you can transfer up to $1,700 onto your Visa® and up to $2,750 onto your Discover® card without exceeding a 30 percent utilization rate.

$\leq$ = *less than or equal to*

OPTION B: PAY OFF ANY DEBTS THAT PUT YOUR BALANCE ABOVE 30 PERCENT OF THE LIMIT.

Paying debt above 30 percent of your balance is often easier said than done. But if you are able, you should consider this option. Be careful not to cause financial strain. If you pay down your debt too aggressively, you might end up struggling to make future payments because you have exhausted your savings. A healthy savings account is especially critical if you are trying to qualify for a home loan, which will require a down payment. Instead of spending all your savings to lower your utilization rate, try to raise your credit limit (Option C).

OPTION C: ASK YOUR CREDIT CARD COMPANY TO INCREASE YOUR LIMIT SO THAT YOUR BALANCE IS LESS THAN 30 PERCENT.

If you cannot pay off excess balances completely or transfer balances above 30 percent to other cards, try asking your credit card company to raise your limit. This too might be easier said than done; after all, keeping your balance below 30 percent of your limit requires that you have a limit 3.34 times the current balance. If you already have a high balance, your credit card company might be hesitant to increase your limit by more than 300 percent! I went from a $20,000 limit to a $60,000 limit by providing income documentation, so I know it can be done, but it will require substantial documentation. The more likely scenario is that you will negotiate a small increase, bringing you closer to your 30 percent goal.

Before making the request, you should ask the creditor three questions and be strategic about moving forward. The answers to these questions will determine how you move forward:

1. **"DO I QUALIFY FOR A LIMIT INCREASE WITHOUT HAVING YOU RUN MY CREDIT REPORT?"** If you do, move on to the next question. If the creditor insists on running your credit report, remember that your score will be dinged, which might be a problem if your credit is borderline. Depending on the number of inquiries you have in the past 12 months, you might not want to request a new inquiry.

2. **"CAN I REQUEST THE MAXIMUM INCREASE, OR MUST I PROVIDE YOU WITH A SPECIFIC LIMIT REQUEST?"** If the creditor requires that you provide a dollar figure to which you want your limit increased, you will need to ask the third question. If not, request the maximum increase.

3. **"IF I REQUEST TOO MUCH, WILL YOU DENY THE REQUEST COMPLETELY, OR WILL YOU MAKE A COUNTEROFFER?"** If asking for too much means the creditor will deny the request completely, you might want to start by requesting a 10 percent or 20 percent increase. If the creditor will make a counteroffer, request the full amount you need to raise your limit enough that your balance is less than 30 percent.

If your limit is raised, remember to keep your balance the same as it was prior to the limit increase. Don't make the mistake of seeing your increased limit as an opportunity to go on a spending spree, thereby failing to reach your goal of a 30 percent utilization rate. Sadly, once a creditor has granted one request for an increased limit, it isn't as likely to grant a second.

If your request is denied, or if it is not raised enough to get you to that magic 30 percent number, stop incurring new debt. If this is not an option, or if you are overextended, then you need to control your spending. Some consumers have a difficult time with this. For those people, I suggest seeking advice from a financial planner or joining a support group for people with spending problems. For a referral, call **(877) 720-SCORE.**

Finally, start paying down your credit balance as much as possible by creating a budget (as explained in **STEP 7**). Again, do not incur new debt. Rather, make your payments on time for six months and then request a limit increase.

Option D: Open another credit card account and transfer balances accordingly (but only after reading Step 2)

If you have less than five credit cards, you might want to consider opening another credit card and transferring a portion of your balances to the new card, as detailed in Option A. Remember that opening a new credit card will lower your score for two reasons: First, new inquiries count against your credit score. New lines of credit also shorten your credit history and therefore lower your credit score. That said, sometimes you must hurt your score to help your score: credit scoring bureaus will give you a higher credit score if you have at least three credit cards.

Keeping this in mind, Option D is a good choice if you fit into one of two categories: 1) you have fewer than three credit cards; or 2) you have fewer than five credit cards, you have credit cards with a utilization rate that exceeds 30 percent, and you have completed the other six steps without seeing your credit score increase substantially.

Regardless, read Step 2 before deciding to open a new line of credit.

If you decide to open a new credit card account, do not transfer the balance at the same time as opening the credit card. Most creditors will determine your balance by the credit transfer you request. If you transfer $5,000, the creditor will give you a $5,000 credit limit and your utilization rate on the new card will be 100 percent. Instead, think strategically. Open the account first and transfer balances from other credit cards only after you have determined the limit and calculated the utilization rate. Remember to transfer no more than 30 percent of the balance onto the new card.

If you have more than five credit cards, **do not** open another account. Instead, complete the remaining six steps and try to lower your utilization rate by revisiting OPTION A, OPTION B, and OPTION C.

How is the Utilization Rate Determined on Cards with Unlimited Balances?

Some credit card companies (e.g., many American Express® accounts) provide cards with no preset spending limit. So how is your utilization rate determined on these cards?

On such cards, credit bureaus report your credit limit using the highest balance you have ever had on your credit card (called the "high credit limit"). Let's consider the following example, which details the 12-month history of a card with an unlimited balance.

Jan	Feb	Mar	Apr	May	Jun	Jul	Aug	Sep	Oct	Nov	Dec
Card open $0 balance	$6,000	$3,000	$5,000	$2,000	$1,500	$3,000	$3,500	$3,750	$4,000	$2,500	$3,250

In this example, the credit card company would report your credit limit as $6,000, your de facto high credit limit, which occurred in February. This means your target 30 percent balance would be $1,800 ($6,000 x 30% = $1,800), a figure you exceeded in nine of 10 subsequent months.

If you must use such a card, avoid exceeding your target utilization rate on these cards by employing the following tactic: spend one month "hiking up" your balance as much as possible, thereby increasing the high credit limit (highest balance) to a high enough mark that you do not exceed the 30 percent utilization rate in subsequent months. I do not recommend that you make unnecessary expenditures to increase your credit limit; rather, transfer your method of payment from cash, check, or alternate credit cards for one month. Choose a time when you can afford to temporarily lower your score, which will occur due to the increased utilization rate. Then, pay your balance in full and start using the card modestly.

A Word
of Caution

Some borrowers are shocked to find that the credit card companies lower limits when consumers lower their utilization rate. Generally, this happens when borrowers have "maxed out" their credit cards and made delinquent payments. If you have a history of maxing out your credit cards and making late payments, or if your credit score has recently dropped, your credit card company might decide that you are high risk and lower your credit limit. However, a credit card company cannot legally lower your limit until you have paid down your balance (otherwise, your credit report would show that you are over the limit, you would be assessed an over-the-limit fee, and your utilization rate would exceed 100 percent).

Therefore, some credit card companies simply wait for the borrower to lower the balance and then lower the credit limit accordingly. If you are a victim of lowered limits, you will need to reduce your balance even more than you originally thought so that your utilization rate reflects the adjusted limit.

Also beware that if you do not use your credit cards regularly, the limit might be lowered. To keep this from happening, keep your credit cards active. Otherwise, your utilization rate will increase in concert with the lowered limit.

KEY POINTS

STEP 1: KEEP YOUR CREDIT CARD BALANCES UNDER 30 PERCENT OF YOUR CREDIT LIMIT.

To increase or maintain your credit score, your balance on any one credit card should be no more than 30 percent of your limit. For instance, if you have a $10,000 spending limit on your Visa® card, keep your balance at no more than $3,000, even if you pay your credit cards in full each month. The debt you carry on a credit card in proportion to your balance is called a "utilization rate," and credit bureaus respond more favorably if your utilization rate is low.

If your utilization rate is too high, you should do one or more of the following:

1. Transfer funds among your credit cards so that each card has a 30 percent balance or less; and/or

2. Pay off any debts that put your balance above 30 percent of the limit; and/or

3. Ask your credit card company to increase your limit so that your balance is less than 30 percent; and/or

4. Open another credit card account and transfer balances accordingly (but only after reading STEP 2).

If you have a credit card with no preset spending limit (like many American Express® cards), credit bureaus report your credit limit using the highest balance you have ever had on your credit card (called the "high credit limit"). This throws your utilization rate out of whack if you generally spend the same amount from month to month. To avoid exceeding your target utilization rate on these cards, you can try this tactic: spend one month "hiking up" your balance as high as possible, thereby increasing the high credit limit (highest balance) to a high enough mark that you do not exceed the 30 percent utilization rate in subsequent months.

KEY POINTS   continued

I do not recommend that you make unnecessary expenditures to increase your credit limit; rather, transfer your method of payment from cash, check, or alternate credit cards for one month. Choose a time when you can afford a temporary setback in your score. Then, pay your balance in full and start using the card modestly.

Visit WWW.7STEPSTO720.COM to learn more about utilization rates.

step*2*

Have at Least Three
Revolving Credit Lines

KASEY AND MICHELLE

Kasey and Michelle had been best friends since the first grade. They both wanted to be journalists and were excited to be rooming together at the same college.

Secretly, Kasey thought Michelle was a bit spoiled. The summer before their junior year in high school, Michelle's parents made her an authorized user on their account and gave her a credit card! Kasey could not believe it. Her parents would never do something so irresponsible.

When Michelle first got her credit card, she misused it a few times. Her parents paid the bill but did not take the card away. Instead, they made Michelle get a job so that she could pay them back. Michelle was hired to deliver newspapers.

In college, Kasey spent all of her time studying. By then, Michelle had applied for her own credit cards and needed to find work to pay the bills. She ended up with two jobs: one working on the school newspaper and another in the tutoring department. Her grades suffered a bit, but Michelle still graduated with a better-than-average GPA.

Kasey was glad her parents had advised her to wait until she graduated from college to apply for a credit card. She ignored the credit card offers that came in the mail. She studied hard and graduated with the highest honors possible.

After graduation, Kasey and Michelle applied for the same job at a prestigious newspaper, the same one that hired Michelle as a delivery girl years earlier. Kasey was shocked when only Michelle was hired. The newspaper's recruiters explained that they were impressed with Michelle's work history and, while Kasey's grades were better, they felt a proven, relevant work history was far more important. Kasey was disappointed, but she waited a few months and got a job in a different department at the same newspaper.

Finally, Kasey was earning a decent salary. She decided to apply for one credit card, but was stunned by the 19 percent interest rate. She asked Michelle what interest rate she carried on her credit cards. Michelle said she had an 8 percent interest rate or less on all three of her cards. Kasey couldn't understand the disparity in their interest rates but decided she would use her credit card responsibly for a while and see what happened. For five years she used her card for emergencies only.

Then Michelle bought a house. It was big and spacious, in a nice neighborhood, and much nicer than anything Kasey had ever thought possible for her friend. But if Michelle could do it, she thought, then why couldn't Kasey?

Kasey had to go through several lenders to find one that would approve her loan. And again, the interest rate was sky high. The lender explained that her relatively limited credit history translated into a high interest rate. Kasey learned an important lesson—again: her friend's credit track record was rewarded favorably, and Kasey's cautious use of one card had not produced good credit but instead had done the opposite.

C redit bureaus award higher scores to people with at least three revolving accounts. (Ideally, bureaus want you to have three to five credit cards.) For the purposes of the **7 STEPS**, consider revolving accounts to be the four major credit cards—Visa®, MasterCard®, American Express®, and Discover®. Though retail accounts, such as a Macy's® card, do affect your credit score, focus on the major revolving cards, which are the ones most consumers use for making purchases.

Why three? Lenders want to be assured that you will not abuse your credit privileges. If you have too many accounts, they figure you have the opportunity to overextend yourself; on the other hand, if you have too few, they don't have proof that you can properly manage multiple accounts.

So if you have fewer than three revolving credit accounts, you should open some new credit cards.

Things to Keep in Mind
When Opening New Accounts

Your bankcard (also known as a check card, a debit card, or an ATM card) is not a credit card, even if it is emblazoned with the Visa® or MasterCard® logo. Bankcards draw against money that exists in your bank account, so they have no bearing on your ability to manage credit.

If you do not plan on carrying a balance from month to month, look for a credit card without an annual fee. Because you will not be carrying a balance, the interest rate will not matter, so choose a card with a higher interest rate and no annual fee over a card with a lower interest rate and an annual fee.

If you do plan on carrying a balance, you should prioritize your interest rate over your annual fee. Savings realized with a low interest rate will make up for the annual fee (generally $29 to $59).

The older the account, the more it affects your credit score constructively. If you have inactive accounts, try reactivating them. This will positively affect your credit more than opening a new account. You will continue benefiting from the account's age, and you will not suffer the credit drop that occurs when opening a new credit card. Be aware that some creditors give their employees bonuses each time they open a new account. Therefore, when you call to have an account reactivated, make sure the representative is reactivating an old account, not opening a new one.

If you need to open more than one credit card account, open them all at once. Though your score might suffer from having several inquiries, in the long run your score will be better off. Eventually, the credit inquiries will drop from your credit report. However, because the longevity of your credit history is a huge factor in determining your credit score, each time you open a credit card, the new account shortens the average credit history and lowers your score. For this reason, open them all at once and get it over with.

For more help finding the right credit card, look online for low-interest rate credit cards, secured credit cards, and cards available for people with poor or no credit. There, you will find a wide range of cards available, such as: low-interest rate credit cards, credit cards with rewards or no annual fee, fixed-rate credit cards, credit cards for borrowers with bad credit, credit cards for students, credit cards for businesses, secured credit cards, and pre-paid credit cards.

If your score is too low, you might find it difficult to open new credit card accounts. In this case, you should try one or both of the following: 1) open a secured credit card; or 2) have someone add you as an authorized user on an existing account.

SECURED CREDIT CARDS

Lenders who offer secured credit cards will require you to make a deposit equal to or more than your limit, thereby "securing" your loan with cash. If you do not make your monthly payment, the deposit eventually will be applied toward your balance. As well, your credit will be damaged upon first delinquency.

Obviously, secured credit cards do not come with the same privileges as regular credit cards, which allow you to buy now, pay later. With secured credit cards, you basically pay now, buy later, and then pay again. It might not sound like a great deal, but a lot of companies will transfer your secured credit card account to a regular credit card after six to 18 months of timely payments, depending on your credit score (the higher your score, the less probationary time needed to obtain an unsecured card). When shopping around for a secured credit card, make sure this is an option. You should also be sure the secured credit card company will report the account to all three credit bureaus. If it will not, don't bother opening the account as it will have no affect on your credit score.

In short, find a secured credit card company that will both report the account to the credit bureaus and issue you a regular, unsecured credit card after you have six to 18 months of timely payments under your belt.

AUTHORIZED USERS

One of the fastest and most powerful ways to increase your credit score is to have a family member or loved one add your name as an authorized user on an existing credit account. By becoming an authorized user, you will benefit from the positive standing of the credit account by "borrowing" a person's credit as associated with the account.

Pablo, a client who emigrated from Mexico, can testify to this. When Pablo became an American citizen, he had a new Social Security card but no credit. His score was 0. In 30 days, his credit score increased to 649 points, in part by being added as an authorized user to two accounts!

To become an authorized user, do both of the following: 1) persuade the account holder to add your name; and 2) choose the right account.

If you have a poor credit history, friends and family members might be reluctant to add your name as an authorized user. To help convince them, explain that the account holder does not need to give you a physical credit card—rather, he will add you in name only. This way, the account holder's good credit can be protected and you won't have an opportunity to mishandle the account. Assure the person that his credit score will not be affected by adding your name unless you misuse the account. Of course, if you do not have a credit card to misuse, this won't be a problem. If the account holder is concerned that your negative credit history might be merged with his credit history, assure the person that this will not happen. Rather, the account holder's positive credit history on this one account will be merged into your credit history, therefore helping your credit score and protecting the account holder's credit score.

Leveraging another person's credit history will be successful only if his credit history on the account to which you are being added is positive. If you are added as an authorized user to an account that is in bad standing, your credit will suffer instead of surge. In other words, find someone with a credit card in good standing and with a less than 30 percent utilization rate on that credit card. When being added to the account, you also will need to make sure that the credit card company reports authorized users to the credit bureaus. If the company does not ask for your Social Security number, it likely won't report to the credit bureaus. Even if the creditor does ask for your Social Security number, you cannot be sure that it will report to the credit bureaus unless you ask. If the credit representative says the account will not be added to your credit report, find another account.

As an authorized user, you run the risk of having the account holder default and damage your credit score. If this happens and your credit score drops lower than it was prior to being added as an authorized user, you should have your name removed immediately from the account. Within 45 days of doing so, your report will stop including the derogatory account.

Maintaining Your Credit Cards

Once you have opened your new credit card accounts, be sure to use no more than 30 percent of your available credit (see STEP 1). You might get a low interest rate and decide to transfer your balance (or a portion thereof) from a higher rate card, being careful not to exceed the 30 percent threshold on the new account. One way or another, you will need to make sure you are using your new card. An inactive account does nothing for your credit. This does not mean that you should make unnecessary purchases just to use the card. Rather, pay a utility bill or your insurance premium using your new credit card and then pay the balance monthly.

What if You Have More Than Three Credit Cards?

Ideally, you should have between three and five credit cards. If you have more than five revolving credit card accounts, you have more opportunities to get into a financial bind than someone with only three or four credit cards. However, do not close extra accounts! Closing them might hurt your score, and it will never help you score.

Instead, show the credit bureaus that you are managing all of your accounts by keeping your utilization rate well below 30 percent.

KEY POINTS

STEP 2: HAVE AT LEAST THREE REVOLVING CREDIT LINES.

Credit bureaus give higher scores to people with at least three revolving credit card accounts, which include major credit cards (i.e., Visa®, MasterCard®, American Express®, and Discover®). If you do not have at least three active credit cards, you should open some.

If you have poor credit, you might not be able to open a typical credit card. In this case, consider opening a secured credit card (see **WWW.7STEPSTO720.COM/FAQ** for links to secured credit cards). Lenders that offer secured credit cards will require you to make a deposit that is equal to or more than your limit, thereby guaranteeing the bank that you will repay the loan. If you do not make your monthly payment, the deposit is applied toward your balance.

Another option for borrowers with poor credit is to be added to an existing account in good standing. In fact, having a friend or family member add you as an **authorized user** is one of the fastest ways to boost your score.

If you have more than three credit card accounts, do not close the accounts. Most credit experts agree that once you have opened the excess accounts, the damage is done. In fact, closing them might hurt your score and will never help it.

step 3

Verify the Accuracy of Your Reported Credit Limits

Here is a little secret: credit card companies are not interested in making your life better. Sure, they have glossy advertisements showing relaxed, happy vacationers using their Visa® cards while dining in luxurious, romantic restaurants. But the truth is they don't really care whether you are vacationing in France or working the night shift making minimum wage to cover your credit card bills. They want to make money. It's not a bad goal, but it can be contrary to yours, which is to save money.

To make money, credit card companies need customers. Once they have customers, they need to keep them. Nothing is more annoying to a credit card company than losing a client to a competitor with a lower rate. So, they have a nasty little trick: they do not always report your proper credit card limits.[1] In fact, a man from South Carolina recently filed a class-action lawsuit against the three major credit bureaus for allowing credit card companies to omit or inaccurately report credit card limits.[2]

Failing to accurately report limits is widespread among credit card companies. Indeed, borrowers with certain major credit cards can be fairly sure that their limits have been withheld from credit bureaus. One credit card company that markets to people with poor credit scores refuses to submit credit limits to Equifax, Experian, or TransUnion. A recent Federal Reserve Board study of more than 300,000 consumers found that 46 percent were missing at least one credit limit on their credit reports.

It works like this: credit card companies buy lists of borrowers whose limits are, for example, more than $10,000. The companies then send credit card offers, often with enticingly low interest rates, to those people on the list. Their goal is to encourage borrowers to switch cards. Needless to say, your credit card company does not want your name on that list. They want to make sure that you remain a loyal customer. In an effort to keep you as a client, some credit card companies report a lower credit limit than you actually have, or they do not report your limit at all. This makes you less appealing to other credit card companies.

And it is bad news for your credit score. If your report is not showing your proper limits, your utilization rate appears out of whack, your credit

---

1. For more information, refer to Kenneth R. Harney's December 25, 2004 *Washington Post* article titled, "Credit Card Limits Often Unreported."
2. See Kenneth R. Harney's July 31, 2006 *Los Angeles Times* article titled, "Class-Action Suit Is Taking on National Credit-Reporting Bureaus."

score is lower, and you are saddled with correspondingly higher interest rates. As you know, the amount of money you owe in relation to your credit limit (your utilization rate) accounts for 30 percent of your overall credit score. Having the incorrect credit limit reported on your credit report can lower your score drastically. This translates into higher interest rates and heftier monthly payments (sometimes increasing a mortgage payment by thousands of dollars).

What if Your Credit Card Company Does Not Report Your Limit?

Having no limit reported is just as damaging as having the wrong limit reported. When this occurs, the credit bureaus usually substitute your highest balance to date in lieu of your actual limit. Other times, your credit report might show a $0 limit! This is dangerous because it will result in an increased utilization rate, especially if you tend to spend the same amount each month on your credit card. For instance, if you have a $10,000 limit on your credit card and your highest balance is $3,250, credit bureaus will list $3,250 as your limit if your credit card company fails·to report your actual $10,000 limit. If you normally carry a $3,000 balance, lenders will think your utilization rate is approximately 92 percent, far exceeding the 30 percent ideal balance described in STEP 1. In other words, regardless of whether you have lowered your balance to 30 percent, the credit bureaus will act as though you are using nearly your entire limit each month, which will drastically reduce your credit score.

This is particularly important for American Express® cardholders, who generally do not have limits, but who are required to pay their balance in full each month. As we discussed earlier, credit bureaus report your American Express® limit as the highest balance you have ever had, again making your utilization rate appear much higher than it likely is.

If you have an American Express® card, you can do one of two things.

The first option is to make all purchases, including those you usually pay for with cash or other credit cards, using your American Express® card during one billing cycle, raising your reported limit as high as you can. In subsequent months, spend no more than 30 percent of the high balance, keeping your utilization rate at the ideal level.

This will work only if you can afford to improve your credit slowly. It requires you to sacrifice your credit score for one month while you raise the reported limit. During this month, your utilization rate will be more than 100 percent! However, in subsequent months, your credit score will improve as your utilization rate declines.

A faster approach to better credit, the second option, is to simply stop using your American Express® card during the months preceding a major purchase. If you must, use it for emergencies only and keep the balance as low as possible.

In short, check your credit report. If your credit limit is not listed, or if it is inaccurate, contact your credit card company and ask it to correct the mistake. Follow up with the credit card company by sending a letter similar to the form "Incorrect Credit Limit Letter for Credit Card Companies" on the **7 Steps** website (**www.7StepsTo720.com/forms**) or in **Applying the 7 Steps to a 720 Credit Score Workbook**. If you are still having problems getting the proper limit reported, contact the credit bureaus directly, send copies of your statements, and ask again that they make the proper corrections. Legally, neither credit bureaus nor credit card companies are required to report your limit. In my experience, most will do so nonetheless if you simply ask, especially in light of the pending class-action lawsuit.

KEY POINTS

STEP 3: VERIFY THE ACCURACY OF YOUR REPORTED CREDIT LIMITS.

Credit card companies often fail to report your credit limit, or they report a lower limit than you have. This causes your utilization rate (see **STEP 1**) to be reported as higher than it actually is, which degrades your credit score.

Why do credit card companies fail to report correct credit limits? They do not want to lose their client base. If other companies see that you have a high limit and a positive credit score, they might solicit your business. By failing to report the correct credit limit, credit card companies keep your name off mailing lists and better retain your business.

If your credit limit is not listed on your credit report, or if it is inaccurate, contact your credit card company and ask it to correct the mistake. Follow up with the credit card company by sending a letter similar to the form "Incorrect Credit Limit Letter for Credit Card Companies" on the **7 STEPS** website (**WWW.7STEPSTO720.COM/FORMS**) or in the **APPLYING THE 7 STEPS TO A 720 CREDIT SCORE WORKBOOK**. If you are still having problems getting the proper limit reported, contact the credit bureaus directly, send copies of your statements, and ask that they make the proper corrections.

step4

Have at Least One Helpful Active or Paid Installment Loan on Your Credit Report

C redit bureaus want to see a healthy mix of credit, so adding a helpful installment loan to your credit report will help maximize your score.

BREEANNA

Remember Breeanna, the frugal spender from the first chapter who paid for everything with cash? When Breeanna came to me, her credit score was 530. Breeanna had very little credit, but she had never missed a credit card payment.

At the time, Breeanna was driving a 1983 Chevrolet Chevette, yet she was making $97,000 a year and had nearly $300,000 in savings. I could tell Breeanna would make an excellent borrower if only she knew the rules of the credit game.

Breeanna and I discussed her dilemma. She wanted to buy a conservative house without depleting her savings. For the first time in her life, Breeanna was willing to become a borrower. Sadly, she needed a credit history to get credit, and a 530 score was going to give her an unacceptably high interest rate.

Breeanna and I discussed her options. I finally convinced her to buy a car using an installment loan. She asked her fiancé to cosign, and Breeanna purchased a 2004 Scion A® with a conservative interest rate.

Initially, because of the recent lender inquiry, Breeanna's score fell a few points. I explained that she needed to take a step back to take two steps forward. She began rebounding immediately. First, her score increased just a few points, but six months later, her score had increased drastically. By opening additional credit card accounts and making her installment loan payments on time, Breeanna's score eventually increased even more, and she was able to purchase her dream home. Today, Breeanna has higher than a 750 credit score, well above the threshold for premium interest rates.

An installment loan is a purchase agreement whereby the borrower repays the loan in equal periodic payments and the loan is secured through a piece of property. Cars, boats, furniture, and computers are typical items bought through installment loans. A car lease is another type of installment loan.

As discussed in previous chapters, the type of credit you have accounts for 15 percent of your credit score, and the bureaus want to see a healthy mix of credit. By now, you know that ideally you should have three major credit cards. Eventually you will qualify for a mortgage loan; for now, work on getting an installment loan.

But beware: installment loans come in two forms. One is helpful, the other harmful.

Helpful installment loans are those that require payment within 30 days of purchasing the item. Harmful installment loans (e.g., finance accounts) are those that delay payment for more than 30 days, as discussed in the **CREDIT FACTS** chapter. For instance, if you purchase a television in June and are not required to make your first payment until January of the following year, you are hurting your credit score instead of helping it. These types of installment loans suggest that you are in a financial bind and cannot afford to make immediate payments. Never apply for these types of loans unless you can afford to see your credit score drop.

If you do not already have an installment loan, or if you have a paid installment loan that is detrimental to your score (e.g., you had many late payments or your car was repossessed), you will need to pay close attention to this chapter. Responsible payment of an installment loan is an excellent way to improve your credit score. Make sure you are committed to keeping your installment loan in good standing. You must pay it on time, every time.

Paying an installment loan is a big obligation, so if this makes you uncomfortable, consider completing all the other steps and reevaluating your plan. You might be able to avoid this step if you are successful in improving your credit using the other six steps. However, failing to have an installment loan on your credit report limits how deeply your credit roots will grow, so consider this carefully.

If you currently have an installment loan, or if you have recently paid one off that is in good standing, you can skip this step. Likewise, if you don't have an installment loan on your credit report, but you already have a high score, you can disregard this step. Your good score can be enhanced using the other steps described in this book.

However, if you have bad credit, especially if you have a paid installment loan that is not in good standing, you will need to add an installment loan to your credit report. To do so, consider the following options:

❖ If you own a car that you bought outright with cash, you can take out a small installment loan ($1,000) using your automobile as collateral. You can do this at your local bank or online. (Visit **WWW.7STEPSTO720.COM/FAQ** for links to lenders online.) *Remember, the purpose of this book is to improve your credit. Taking out an installment loan on a car that has been paid for might not be in your immediate best financial interest. However, it will improve your credit rating, which translates to lower interest rates on future credit cards, mortgages, installment loans, etc.*

❖ If you are in the market for a new or used car, take out an installment loan, even if you have the means to pay for the car in full. Shop around at your local bank and online to find the best loan. The size of the loan doesn't necessarily matter nor does the length of the loan. What is most important is showing the credit bureaus that you can pay on time without defaulting. If you are uncomfortable taking out a large installment loan, borrow a small amount of money and pay it back immediately. (Remember that lenders will count all inquiries into a car loan that occur within a 45-day period as just one inquiry.)

❖ If you need furniture, a computer, or other large household appliances, you might consider purchasing them through an installment loan. Many stores offer such loans, but shoppers should be aware that it is sometimes difficult to tell whether they are purchasing items through a retail account (a store-specific credit card) or through an installment loan. Be sure to ask. Also, make sure that you are not applying for a finance account, which is a harmful installment loan.

Jake

Jake had impeccable credit. He paid his bills on time and in full. He had three major credit cards, each with a utilization rate less than 30 percent. He had an automobile loan and had never missed a payment. His credit score was 759.

But Jake's spending habits were less than conservative. Jake never saved a dime, always knowing the next paycheck would come in just two weeks.

Then he lost his job unexpectedly. He panicked. How was he going to pay his bills? Sure, he could pay rent, the utilities, and his cell phone bill. He could probably swing the minimum payments on his credit cards, but his car payment was just going to have to wait.

Jake's score didn't budge the first month. After all, the credit bureaus don't consider a payment late until 30 days past the due date. The second month, his score dropped significantly, and it kept falling. By the third month, his car was repossessed, and his score fell again. Suddenly, he had a subprime credit score.

The moral of this story: once you have an installment loan on your credit report, pay it on time every time. As helpful as an installment loan can be to your credit rating, it can be equally harmful if it is not paid on time.

KEY POINTS

STEP 4: HAVE AT LEAST ONE HELPFUL ACTIVE OR PAID INSTALLMENT LOAN ON YOUR CREDIT REPORT.

Having a healthy mix of credit is a great way to increase your credit score. Therefore, to maximize your credit score you should have at least one installment loan, a mortgage, and three major revolving credit cards (Visa®, MasterCard®, American Express®, or Discover®). Typically, an installment loan is used to purchase a car, but it also can be used to purchase a computer, furniture, or major household appliances.

If you do not have an installment loan on your credit report, you should consider adding one. You can visit your bank to take out a small installment loan on an existing vehicle or, if you are in the market for household appliances, consider purchasing them using an installment loan.

Make your installment payments on time. As helpful as an installment loan can be to your credit rating, it can be equally harmful if not paid on time.

Beware of harmful installment loans—those that delay payment on an item for more than 30 days. This type of credit will always hurt and never help your credit score.

For links to lenders who can provide you with an installment loan for your automobile, visit **WWW.7STEPSTO720.COM/FAQ.**

step5

Remove High-Priority Errors from Your Credit Report

This one seems obvious. Of course you should check your credit report for errors! You might be thinking, *I doubt I have any mistakes on my credit report.* Think again. Approximately 80 percent of all credit reports have at least one error[1]. The worst errors—those caused by identity theft—can be a nightmare to remove from your credit report. Even simple, honest errors can be challenging and time-consuming.

However, don't get carried away correcting every error on your credit report. Concentrate only on significant errors, those that occurred less than two years ago. Because credit scoring formulas place more weight on recent activities than past activities, an error that occurred less than two years ago can be two or three times more damaging than an error that occurred five years ago.

What Is an Error?

An error can be as simple as having the wrong address or name listed on an account. It can be a limit that is not listed, or accounts you do not own. Among the most damaging are errors that occur in credit reports with items in collection. People with accounts that have been sent to a collection agency often have duplicate active collection notices reported for the same account.

This chapter details the errors you might find on your credit report and offers suggestions for correcting them. A word of warning about this chapter: remember that you should not waste your valuable time trying to correct every mistake on your credit report. Concentrate on high-priority errors that occurred within the past two years. Some books suggest that you spend countless hours writing letters to credit bureaus and creditors trying to remove derogatory items from your credit report. Though the accompanying workbook (available at **WWW.7STEPSTO720.COM**) has provided all the forms necessary for such letters, the **7 STEPS** process works best if you concentrate on more efficient, less time-consuming activities that will boost your credit score.

---

1. 2004 U.S. Public Interest Research Group Survey.

Types of Errors You Might Find on Your Credit Report

DUPLICATES

❖ Active collection accounts less than two years old and listed more than once (high priority).

❖ Other account information listed more than once (high priority if the account is harming your credit; low priority if it is helping your credit).

PERSONAL INFORMATION

❖ Someone else's Social Security number or a mistake in your Social Security number (high priority as it could indicate that you are a victim of identity fraud, or it could result in your credit report being merged with another person's report).

❖ Someone else's name or a mistake in your name (high priority as it could indicate that you are a victim of identity fraud, or it could result in your credit report being merged with another person's).

❖ Incorrect address or a mistake in your address (low priority, unless you think you might be a victim of identity fraud, as described later in this step).

❖ Wrong date of birth (low priority, unless you think you might be a victim of identity fraud).

❖ Other incorrect information, such as your employer (low priority).

MISTAKES IN YOUR ACCOUNT INFORMATION

❖ Incorrect account numbers (low priority, unless you think you're a victim of identity fraud).

❖ Incorrect credit limit (high priority).

❖ Mistakes in your payment history (high priority only if the mistake is hurting your credit and occurred within the past two years).

❖ Delinquencies older than seven years (low priority).

❖ Accounts that are not listed in your credit report (high priority only if the accounts help your score).

Information that Doesn't Belong to You

❖ Accounts that are not yours (highest priority as it could indicate that you are a victim of identity fraud).

❖ Collection notices that are not yours (highest priority as it could indicate that you are a victim of identity fraud).

❖ Social Security numbers that are not yours (highest priority as it could indicate that you are a victim of identity fraud).

❖ Names that are not yours (highest priority as it could indicate that you are a victim of identity fraud).

If your credit report has any high-priority errors, start correcting those that are listed as having occurred within the past 24 months. I do not advise that you spend much time correcting low-priority errors, especially those that occurred more than two years ago. Your time is valuable, and the corrections probably will not help your score significantly.

Be aware that you should not correct more than two errors at a time unless you are a victim of identity fraud. You will learn more about this later in this step. For now, just keep it in mind when moving forward.

Correcting Duplicates

Perhaps the most common (and among the most damaging) error on a credit report is a duplicate collection notice. If you notice that more than one collection agency is actively reporting your account, you should work quickly to have this removed.

Accounts turned over for collection, which are often transferred several times among collection companies, show more than once on your credit report because all companies previously and currently trying to collect the debt report the account. This is to be expected. However, if more than one company is **actively** reporting your account, your score will suffer.

MARCUS

To make a long story short, Marcus went through a rough spot. He lost his job, his wife left him, he started drinking heavily, and his finances fell apart. Most of his bills were turned over to collection companies.

But then Marcus recovered. He got a job (and a girlfriend), quit drinking, and started paying his bills on time.

Trying to repair his credit, Marcus started reviewing his credit report. He noticed that two of his accounts in collection were listed several times. What was going on? Shouldn't the account be listed just once?

When a bill is turned over for collection, the original creditor will keep the account on your credit report, noting the delinquent payment history and that the account has been turned over for collection. As well, the collection agencies previously and currently responsible for collecting the debt will list the account. This is to be expected, and there really isn't anything you can (or should) do about it.

However, if multiple collection agencies are reporting that they are **actively** collecting on the same account, you should demand that the duplicate entries be removed. The only entries that should be on the account are: 1) the original creditor's report of the delinquent history and collection status; 2) the collection agencies previously responsible for collecting the debt, who should report the account as transferred or sold; and 3) the collection agency currently responsible for collecting the debt. Only the third entry should be actively reporting to credit bureaus.

A common mistake occurs when one collection agency fails to recover the debt and sells the account to another collection agency. The collection agency that sold the account should either have its listing removed from your credit report or list the account as transferred, sold, or closed. However, this doesn't always happen.

To request that credit bureaus correct duplications, use "Letter Correcting Duplications" at WWW.7STEPSTO720.COM/FORMS or in the accompanying APPLYING THE 7 STEPS TO A 720 CREDIT SCORE WORKBOOK.

Personal Information

If your personal information is incorrect, it might be hurting your credit score—but it likely isn't. If your address is listed as 619 East Main Drive instead of 619 East Main Street, your score is not suffering. Likewise, credit scoring models do not care whether you were born in 1969 or 1970. You can correct this information by writing to the credit bureau (see form "Letter Correcting Personal Information" in APPLYING THE 7 STEPS TO A 720 CREDIT SCORE WORKBOOK or at WWW.7STEPSTO720.COM/FORMS), but this should be a low priority (or not a priority at all). You will learn later that credit bureaus might not investigate your claims if you request too many corrections at once. And again, if you have errors that are hurting your credit score, work on getting them corrected; revisit low-priority mistakes down the road. Or don't. They probably aren't hurting your score.

On the other hand, if someone else's name or Social Security number is on your credit report, you could have a big problem. Is another person's account history being merged with yours? If so, his account history might be negatively influencing your credit score. With any luck, you will not have much of a problem correcting this information. Send as many documents verifying your identity to the credit bureau as you can. For instance, send a copy of your driver's license and your Social Security card, as well as the form letter mentioned above ("Letter Correcting Personal Information") to the credit bureau.

Be alert that another person's Social Security number or address might indicate that you are a victim of identity fraud. We will talk more about identity fraud later in this chapter. For now, know to look for mistakes that are more than mere typos. If an address at which you have never lived is listed on your credit report, you should be on high alert. If it is obvious that the credit bureau or creditor has merely made a typographical error, do not worry too much about it.

Correcting Mistakes in Your Account Information

To identify mistakes in your account information, it helps if you have kept good records. After all, it's not easy to prove you have not made late payments if you do not keep your bank statements, copies of checks, and bills. Some mistakes, such as incorrect account numbers or incorrect credit limits, are easy to spot and simpler to prove.

When looking for mistakes, you should write a list of anything you think might be wrong. High-priority items that you know are wrong should take precedence over those that you cannot prove.

For fastest results, work with your lender to correct mistakes. Some lenders (including me) have tools that allow us to update your credit report within 24 hours, though it would take you 30 to 60 days working alone.

The following list details the types of mistake; it also provides tips on correcting them:

❖ Incorrect credit limit. As discussed in STEP 3, having an incorrect credit limit on your credit report increases your utilization rate and lowers your credit-worthiness. Try to correct this mistake by sending "Incorrect Credit Limit Letter for Credit Card Companies" (found at WWW.7STEPSTO720.COM/FORMS or in APPLYING THE 7 STEPS TO A 720 CREDIT SCORE WORKBOOK). Send the letter, as well as a copy of your credit card statement.

❖ Incorrect account numbers. These mistakes are not likely to be hurting your score, unless the account is not yours, in which case you could be a victim of identity theft (as explained later in this step). To correct inaccurate account numbers, use "Letter Correcting Account Numbers" found at the following web address: WWW.7STEPSTO720.COM/FORMS or in APPLYING THE 7 STEPS TO A 720 CREDIT SCORE WORKBOOK. Along with the letter, enclose copies of your most recent statement showing the correct account number. Be aware that full account numbers do not always appear on your credit report. Rather, the creditor might choose to report only a partial account number. If you have a partial account number listed on your credit report, do not bother requesting that it be corrected. It technically is not wrong and the "correction" will not help your score.

❖ Mistakes in your payment history. Unless you have kept meticulous records for the past seven years, this is likely the hardest mistake to correct. If you notice that you have late payments that you do not remember as being delinquent, provide documentation (checks, bank statements, etc.) that will help you prove your position. Use the "Mistakes in Your Payment History" form letter found at WWW.7STEPSTO720.COM/FORMS or in the accompanying APPLYING THE 7 STEPS TO A 720 CREDIT SCORE WORKBOOK.

❖ Accounts that are not listed in your credit report. If the accounts will help your credit score, you should send a letter ("Request to Add Account" found online at WWW.7STEPSTO720.COM/FORMS or in the accompanying APPLYING THE 7 STEPS TO A 720 CREDIT SCORE WORKBOOK) to request that the credit agency add the account to your credit report. However, know that credit bureaus are under no obligation to include the accounts. They also might charge a fee for this service. You should also try contacting the creditor directly ("Request to Add Account 2" form letter found in the accompanying APPLYING THE 7 STEPS TO A 720 CREDIT SCORE WORKBOOK or at WWW.7STEPSTO720.COM/FORMS).

Correcting Information
that Doesn't Belong to You

If your credit report includes information, such as accounts, names, or Social Security numbers that do not belong to you, you could be a victim of identity theft. We will talk more about identity theft later in this chapter. For now, note that these items should take precedence over any other error on your credit report until you determine whether you are a victim of identity fraud. If you are, put all the other mistakes aside while you work on reclaiming your identity. If you are not a victim of identity fraud, correct the mistake using the "Correcting Information that Does Not Belong to Me" form letter found at **www.7StepsTo720.com/forms** or in the accompanying **Applying the 7 Steps to a 720 Credit Score Workbook**. Again, include any documentation that supports your claim (such as a copy of your Social Security card, driver's license, etc.).

Knowing Your
Rights

Fortunately, consumers are protected by something called the Fair Credit Reporting Act, a set of laws that protects consumers from creditors and credit bureaus incorrectly reporting information. Under this act, you have the right to dispute any item on your credit report that you believe is wrong. In turn, credit agencies must respond to your dispute. (There is a big exception here: creditors do not have to respond to your dispute if they think it is "frivolous".) If they do not respond, you can always sue them. In short, consumers have a lot of protection in this area.

Do not make the mistake of assuming that this process is easy. Be persistent and keep a good paper trail if you want to correct your credit report. The process works like this:

1. Upon identifying an error, you should submit a dispute detailing the item(s) listed incorrectly in your credit report. Send the dispute only to the credit bureaus that have

erroneously reported the item. You can submit disputes on a credit agency's website, which some say is the fastest way of dealing with incorrect information.

TransUnion:	WWW.TRANSUNION.COM
Equifax:	WWW.EQUIFAX.COM
Experian:	WWW.EXPERIAN.COM

You also can submit the dispute through standard mail using the forms at WWW.7STEPSTO720.COM/FORMS or in APPLYING THE 7 STEPS TO A 720 CREDIT SCORE WORKBOOK. When you submit your dispute, also include copies (never send the originals) of documentation supporting your claim. Send all correspondence using certified mail with a return receipt request.

2. Upon receiving the dispute letter, the agency begins the investigation by contacting the creditor. The creditor is required to verify that the item in question is correct, which might be difficult given that some creditors destroy their records every few years.

3. Expect a written response from the credit agency within 30 days. This correspondence will either provide the results of the investigation or request more information, in which case the agency has an additional 15 days to complete its investigation.

4. If you do not hear back in 30 days, give the credit agency the benefit of the doubt and send a second letter requesting that your claim be investigated. If you do not hear back within 30 days on your second try, ask an attorney to write a letter to the credit agency. An attorney's letterhead can be quite powerful when trying to resolve issues.

5. Your credit report will not change if the credit agency finds that the item was reported correctly.

6. If the agency determines that your dispute is valid, or if it cannot verify the disputed item's accuracy, it is required by law to remove (permanently or temporarily) the item you are disputing. In this case, you will also receive a free copy of your corrected credit report. As well, the agency must send your corrected credit report to all creditors and employers who have requested your credit report in the past two years if you so request.

7. A few months after receiving your corrected credit report, you should request another copy of your report so that you can make sure the mistake has not resurfaced. If it has, send the "Resurfacing Letter" (found in the accompanying APPLYING THE 7 STEPS TO A 720 CREDIT SCORE WORKBOOK or at WWW.7STEPSTO720.COM/FORMS) to request that the credit agencies remove that item from your credit report.

If the Credit Agency Does Not Remove the Item from Your Credit Report

If a credit agency refuses to delete an incorrect item from your credit report, you have several avenues. First, you should contact the customer service department of the original creditor. Send a letter requesting that the creditor correct the information (see the "Resurfacing Letter 2" found at WWW.7STEPSTO720.COM/FORMS or in APPLYING THE 7 STEPS TO A 720 CREDIT SCORE WORKBOOK). If the creditor does not respond, follow up with a phone call.

If the creditor resists your request, politely remind the creditor that the Fair Credit Reporting Act requires the creditor to correct inaccurate information with the credit bureaus.

Once you have exhausted all other avenues, consider hiring an attorney to sue the credit agency or creditor. Your attorney can determine whether you should move forward with a lawsuit based on the laws in your state. Remember that laws regarding credit reporting are constantly changing. Therefore, it is wise to consult with an attorney or credit specialist about any questions you might have regarding your unique credit report. For a referral, call **(877) 720-SCORE**.

Suppression Versus Deletion

PAUL

Paul spent several months disputing items on his credit report. Some were actual errors by creditors and credit agencies; others were derogatory items that were listed correctly.

When Paul sent his initial letter of dispute, he detailed 17 items he claimed were incorrect. Of those, only four were actually mistakes.

The credit agencies took one look at his letter and laughed. They had seen scams like this before. Paul incorrectly thought that if he disputed everything negative on his credit report, he could flood the agencies with paperwork and his credit report would be magically repaired.

Paul found out the hard way that it does not work that way. The credit agencies sent him a response saying that they would not investigate his claims. They said his actions were "frivolous." Therefore, the credit agencies were not required under the Fair Credit Reporting Act to investigate.

Paul was crushed. Four of those items were wrong, and now they were going to stay on his credit report!

A few months later, Paul decided to start requesting investigations one at a time. He started by addressing the actual errors on his credit report. Five months later, the credit agencies had each verified that the information was inaccurate, and his credit score began to improve.

One by one, he started disputing the derogatory items that were correct. Paul thought that because most credit card companies don't keep records, he could slowly get the derogatory items deleted from his credit report. And sure enough, the items slowly began falling off his credit report. At the end of the process, Paul had increased his credit score substantially, though it still wasn't quite above 720.

Over the next few months, Paul protected his credit by paying his bills on time and in full each month. He never made a late payment, so he figured there was no need to pull a copy of his credit report. He was sure that it would increase to 720 after two years of timely payments and no new delinquencies.

A year later, Paul found his dream home. He was ready for his first mortgage. He called me and asked to be preapproved for a loan. Paul was dismayed when he found that his credit score had dropped since he last checked it a year ago. The extra interest payments would be astronomical!

Paul and I looked over his credit report and found that five of the items from the credit bureaus' investigations had reappeared on his report. What happened? They had been deleted, right? Why did they come back?

When investigating a dispute, a credit agency suppresses the item under question if it cannot verify its accuracy within 30 days. This means that the item is temporarily removed from your credit report. Do not be fooled by suppressed items. They can rear their ugly heads months later and pop back onto your credit report.

On the other hand, deleted items usually stay off your credit report forever. If a credit agency determines that your dispute was valid, it will delete the item from your credit report. Though a creditor might later verify the item's accuracy, this is rare. Usually, when the credit agency deletes an item, it does so because the creditor made a mistake.

Suppressed items can reappear if your dispute is determined invalid during the investigation. When a credit agency conducts an investigation and is unable to verify an item's accuracy within 30 days, it suppresses the item and gives you the benefit of the doubt. However, if a creditor later verifies the item's accuracy, the credit agency will lift the suppression, meaning the item will reappear on your credit report.

So how do you tell the difference between a suppressed item and a deleted item? Your credit report and credit score initially behave the same way regardless of whether an item is suppressed or deleted. Either way, the item initially does not show up on your credit report, and it does not affect your credit score. To determine whether an item has been suppressed or deleted, you will have to pay attention to the letter from the credit agency regarding its findings of your dispute. If the letter says the item was not verifiable, it has likely been suppressed and can later reappear. If the letter says the item was deleted, you can be fairly certain that the item has been removed from your credit report forever.

If you have suppressed items in your credit history, keep your fingers crossed. Hopefully, the creditor will never verify the item's accuracy. Because of the seven-year rule, it will be a non-issue seven years after the date the derogatory item occurred. Otherwise, you always run the risk of having it reappear.

Note that medical accounts (e.g., hospital bills) have special rules and are suppressed the minute you dispute them. Though medical bills will reappear once verified, credit bureaus do not have a 30-day period to investigate prior to suppression.

"Frivolous" Disputes

Remember Paul, the guy who decided to dispute every derogatory item on his credit report at once? Paul learned the hard way that he should not dispute more than a couple of items at one time. If you send a long list of disputes, credit bureaus will assume you are trying to scam them. Credit bureaus are protected from investigating disputes they deem frivolous, which includes anything that looks like a person is trying to avoid paying for past mistakes.

So even if you are trying to circumvent the rules (which I don't recommend), try to be more clever than Paul. Send your disputes over time in groups of two, and wait for a resolution to each item before submitting any additional disputes.

Identity
Theft

If you are a victim of identity fraud, also known as identity theft, you are not alone. In fact, the Federal Trade Commission reported that nearly 10 million Americans were victims of identity theft in 2002 alone.

On average, identity thieves steal services, money, or goods that cost businesses and consumers more than $50 billion each year. In 2002, the most serious of these thieves obtained an average of $10,200 worth of goods, services, or money by using the victim's information. On average, the victims spent 60 hours resolving their problems, and many spent five or six times this figure.[1]

Statistics show that you will likely be a victim of identity theft sometime in the next 10 years. You could spend hundreds of hours and dollars cleaning up the mess caused by identity theft. You might have a poor credit score, your credit cards could be canceled, and collection companies could start hounding you.

But if you are careful, you might be able to avoid all of this.

Avoiding
Identity Theft

To avoid the repercussions of identity theft, you will need to take some preventive measures. For one, buy a shredder and shred any documents that have sensitive and confidential information (e.g., account information, passwords, Social Security numbers, etc.). If you must keep copies, protect your electronic files by allowing files to be accessed only by passwords, and lock hard copies in a file cabinet or safe. Guests, friends, repairmen, and even family have been known to steal account information from unsuspecting consumers.

For this reason, never give out your passwords or Personal Identification Numbers (PINs), not even to friends or family members. Do not choose obvious passwords (the last four digits of your Social Security number, your pet's name, etc.). You should also use a different password

---

1. January 2005 Federal Trade Commission website (WWW.CONSUMER.GOV/IDTHEFT).

for each account. This will minimize damage if a thief does get one of your passwords. Do not write down your passwords or PINs, and definitely do not carry them in your purse or wallet. If you cannot commit them to memory, store passwords and PINs under lock and key.

Guard your Social Security number as much as possible. Try not to give it out, and do not keep your Social Security number in your wallet. If you lose your wallet, or if it is stolen, your Social Security card will be the most helpful item to a thief. Make the thief's job as challenging as possible and keep your Social Security number, as well as birth certificates and other sensitive information, under lock and key.

Do not make online purchases unless the site being used is secure. If you are not sure, do not make the purchase until you can call the business and verify the site's security. Speaking of phone calls, never give account numbers over the phone unless you have initiated the phone call. If a business calls asking you to verify your account number, ask for the request in writing. Thieves can easily impersonate your bank or your credit card company over the phone.

Distrust e-mails that ask you to verify account or credit card numbers. Do not respond to these e-mails. Simply push delete, even if the e-mail address of the sender looks genuine. Legitimate businesses know never to send sensitive information through e-mail.

Identity fraud can occur through standard postal mail, too. Do not ever put your mail in an unprotected mailbox. Drop it in a protected postal mail drop that cannot be accessed by anyone other than postal employees.

Use your credit cards wisely. Dishonest waiters, cab drivers, and retail store clerks can make the most of the latest technology to actually duplicate your credit card.

Finally, and most important, keep your receipts, review your bank and credit cards statements each month, and check your credit report at least twice a year. If you have good financial records, you will recognize signs of identity fraud more quickly.

Signs You Might Be a Victim
of Identity Theft

Identity theft can take one of two forms:

1. Use of your existing accounts to make purchases or otherwise rack up charges for which you become responsible; or
2. Use of your Social Security number and name to open new credit cards or to take out loans.

Both types are detrimental to your credit, so you need to learn to identify warning signs that you might be a victim of identity theft. Victims of identity theft often do not recognize the warning signs until they have suffered massive debt because of the thief. Learning to recognize the signs can save you a lot of time and money. It can also help preserve your credit.

Following are some of the signs that you are a victim of identity theft:

❖ Your credit card statements show purchases you did not make.

❖ You start receiving calls from creditors or collection companies about accounts you never opened.

❖ You stop receiving your credit card statements.

❖ Your credit report lists accounts that are not yours.

❖ Your cell phone bill has lengthy calls you don't remember making to numbers you don't recognize.

❖ Your personal information (name, address, Social Security number, date of birth, etc.) is incorrect on your credit report.

❖ Your credit card company calls you to let you know of unusual activity on your account.

❖ You receive bills for accounts you did not open.

❖ Your bank balance does not match your records.

❖ Your checking account is overdrawn, showing purchases you do not remember making.

❖ Your creditors did not receive the payments you sent.

What if You Are a Victim of Identity Theft?

The first thing you should do if you think someone has stolen your information is verify that you are a victim of identity theft. Perhaps you have noticed an unauthorized charge on your credit card statement. Immediately call the creditor and request more information. Perhaps it is simply a mistake on behalf of the creditor, or perhaps you did not recognize the name of the vendor.

If you are indeed a victim of identity fraud, cancel the cards in question immediately. Request that the creditor assign you a new account number and issue a new credit card (note that this will not hurt your credit score).

Once you have verified that you are a victim of identity fraud, visit the Federal Trade Commission's website (**WWW.CONSUMER.GOV/IDTHEFT**) and follow its advice:

1. Contact the fraud departments of any one of the three major credit bureaus to place a fraud alert on your credit file. The fraud alert requests creditors to contact you before opening any new accounts or making any changes to your existing accounts. As soon as the credit bureau confirms your fraud alert, the other two credit bureaus will be automatically notified to place fraud alerts, and all three credit reports will be sent to you free of charge.

2. Close the accounts that you know or believe have been tampered with or opened fraudulently. Use the ID Theft Affidavit (available at **WWW.CONSUMER.GOV/IDTHEFT**) when disputing new unauthorized accounts.

3. File a police report. Get a copy of the report to submit to your creditors and others that may require proof of the crime.

4. File your complaint with the FTC. (See **WWW.CONSUMER.GOV/IDTHEFT** for the complainant form.) The FTC maintains a database of identity theft cases used by law enforcement agencies for investigations.

—**WWW.CONSUMER.GOV/IDTHEFT**

You might need to take additional steps, as well. In rare cases, you will need to obtain a new Social Security number, a long and extremely difficult process. If this is the case, contact the Social Security Administration's fraud hotline at **(800) 269-0271**. Finally, contact a credit specialist who can help you save or restore your credit score. Visit www.7StepsTo720.com for a referral.

KEY POINTS

STEP 5: REMOVE HIGH-PRIORITY ERRORS FROM YOUR CREDIT REPORT.

This step might seem obvious, but errors come in all shapes and sizes. In fact, approximately 80 percent of all credit reports have at least one error. The worst errors, those caused by identity theft, can be a nightmare to remove from your credit report. Even simple, honest errors can be challenging and time-consuming. An error can be as simple as having the wrong address or name listed on an account. It can be a limit that is not listed. It could be investments you did not make or accounts you do not own. People with accounts in collection often have duplicate collection notices reported for the same account. Whatever the error, identify it and correct it. By removing erroneous information from your report, you could see your score jump 20, 50, or even 100 points!

Beware, however, of spending too much time on this step. Errors that are older than two years are likely not hurting your credit score that much. As well, you probably should not waste your time correcting low-priority errors. Faster, more efficient ways to increase your credit score are described in the other six steps.

For a referral to a credit specialist who can help you analyze your credit report, call **(877) 720-SCORE**, or visit **WWW.7STEPSTO720.COM**.

step **6**

Negotiate for a Letter of Deletion Before Paying a Bill in Collection

From a credit perspective, paying a bill that has been turned over for collection can be more damaging than ignoring it. As you know from previous chapters, your recent payment history is far more important than your past, more mature payment history. In fact, collection accounts only minimally hurt your score after two years, and after four years, the damage is all but erased. But each time you make a payment on a collection account, it renews the activity, damages your score, and restarts the seven-year period that the item will remain on your credit report. As well, in some states, payments restart the statute of limitations on when the creditor can sue you. For this reason, upon consulting with an attorney or credit specialist, you should stop paying collection bills until you can pay them in full and negotiate for a letter of deletion.

Let's say, for instance, you have a bill that is turned over to a collection company. You do not make any payments on the account until month 30, at which point you make a partial payment. Even though your score increased after month 24, your month 30 payment causes it to drop again. Additionally, the collection activity won't fall off your credit report for seven years after the date of last payment, and in some states (e.g., California) the creditor has four more years in which to sue you. Had you not made the month 30 payment, your credit score would be almost entirely recovered by month 48, and the creditor would no longer be able to sue you. Three years later (seven years after the item was sent to collection), the item would be wiped from your report.

*A paid current collection is **worse** than an unpaid collection over 24 months*

Therefore, before paying a bill that has been turned over for collection, consider negotiating for a letter of deletion. (During your first attempts, you should refrain from admitting that the account belongs to you. We'll discuss this in detail later in this chapter. For now, just remember not to admit guilt!) A letter of deletion is provided to the credit bureaus by a creditor or collection agency asking that a derogatory item be wiped from the consumer's credit report. A **letter of deletion**, which differs drastically from a letter of payment, states that the collection report was an error. By law, upon receiving a letter of deletion, the credit bureaus must remove the negative item, thereby allowing your credit score to increase. Be aware that a **letter of payment** simply alerts the credit bureau that you have paid the collection in full. With a letter of payment, the item still appears on your credit report and still affects your credit score. As a result, a letter of payment is not nearly as powerful as a letter of deletion.

It is your responsibility to pay your debts, but be advised that many credit specialists will tell you to wait to contact a collection company until you can pay off the debt in full. You then have leverage to ask the collection company to provide you with a letter of deletion. If the collection company refuses, you can refuse to pay the debt. Hopefully, with a lot of persistence, you can persuade the collection company to grant your request. After all, the creditor/collection company would rather you pay the bill than not.

Paying off your debt is almost always the right thing to do. But there is a little bit of moral ambiguity here. Most collection activities are a result of failure to pay credit cards. Remember that credit card companies do awful things to their clients, which they get away with only because many consumers cannot get by without credit. We put up with their lousy terms and (sometimes) unethical behavior in exchange for the privilege of borrowing money. If you are feeling bad about negotiating to get a credit card collection notice removed from your bill, remember these things:

1. Some credit card companies send unsolicited credit cards to college students with little or no credit history, no income, and who lack the financial knowledge to handle credit cards

responsibly. Why? They hope that students will make rash purchases, incur debt, rack up huge financing charges with high interest, and then turn to their parents to bail them out. In short, credit card companies prey on those who might have no experience paying even a single bill, much less managing credit responsibly. As a result, many of these students find themselves facing financial hardships and collection notices at the beginning of their adult lives.

2.   Many, if not most, credit card companies have something called the Universal Default Clause, which allows them to charge you a 29.9 percent interest rate (or higher) if you ever make a late payment on any credit card, even if that card isn't one issued by that company. Imagine this: you have four credit cards, all with interest rates of 10 percent or less. Your employer suddenly tells you that he is going out of business and you are without a job. You liquidate some assets and scramble to get your bills paid. Unfortunately, you are late on one credit card: your MasterCard®. The next month, you notice that your MasterCard®, as well as your American Express®, Visa®, and Discover® cards are all charging you a 29.9 percent interest rate. The Universal Default Clause is one of the "fine print" items credit card companies don't want you to know about. Credit card companies periodically pull your credit report and raise your interest rate based on the history of other accounts you maintain. Credit card companies say that they believe your behavior on one credit card might be the same on all credit cards. It's also a way for credit card companies to charge you a high interest rate even if your payment history has been perfect on their credit cards. And it results in high monthly payments that some borrowers find themselves unable to pay.[1]

If you are a victim of either of these scenarios, do not feel bad about insisting on a letter of deletion before paying off a bad debt. Credit card companies often employ sneaky tactics that can bruise your credit and damage your finances; requesting that they help reverse the effects of their actions is not asking too much.

Most items that go through the collection process fall into one of two categories: collection and charge-offs. In the first stage, **collection**, the original creditor (e.g., Visa®) still wants to collect 100 percent of your debt but has hired an outside collection company to handle all communications with you, the borrower. When and if you pay, the original creditor (in this case, Visa®) will receive the majority of the outstanding debt. The collection company will receive either a flat fee or a small percentage of the amount it successfully collects from you.

Under the second scenario, charge-offs, the original creditor (e.g., Visa®) has given up all hope of collecting the debt from you. The creditor has "written off" the debt from its books. This is called a **charge-off**, and it generally occurs after a borrower has failed to pay a bill for six months. In this case, the original creditor (Visa®) has sold the account to a collection company for pennies on the dollar. For instance, if your outstanding debt to Visa® is $5,763, Visa® might sell this account for about $500 to a collection company, which will then keep 100 percent of whatever it collects from you, even if it collects the full $5,763 that was owed to Visa®. Once an account has been charged-off, the original creditor no longer has anything to do with the account.

With such a huge profit potential, it is no wonder collection companies so relentlessly pursue debtors.

If you have consulted with a specialist and decided to negotiate for a letter of deletion, you need to first determine whether your bad debt is in the collection phase or the charge-off phase. To determine this, review your credit report to see if the original creditor lists the account as a "charge-off."

If your debt is in the collection phase, negotiate with the original creditor. If your debt is in the charge-off phase, negotiate with the collection company.

Negotiating with a Creditor
for a Letter of Deletion

Before you begin the negotiation process, determine how much you can realistically pay. Preferably, you can pay the entire debt. The more you can pay, the more leverage you have. Whatever that amount is, figure it out before you contact the creditor. Good salesmen know that they should start negotiating with a smaller figure than their maximum. Regardless of where you start negotiating, identify your end point ahead of time. If you are pressured into paying a larger amount than you can realistically pay and you default, you could hurt your credit even more.

Be prepared for the creditor to be a nasty person. Though this is not always the case, if you prepare for the worst, the actual call will not be as traumatic. The creditor will likely act disappointed in you, mad at you, or treat you as though you have harmed him personally. Tell yourself that no matter how the creditor acts, you will remain calm. Most creditors will warm up when they realize that you truly want to pay the debt.

You also should prepare a script. See the script ("Script") found at WWW.7STEPSTO720.COM/FORMS or in the APPLYING THE 7 STEPS TO A 720 CREDIT SCORE WORKBOOK. Obviously, once you start talking to a live person, you will deviate slightly from your script. Your script is intended to remind you that you have a goal: to raise your credit score. Basically, the creditor will say one of three things: 1) yes, it will provide you with a letter of deletion; 2) no, it will not provide you with a letter of deletion; or 3) it will provide you with a letter of payment. The last two scenarios amount basically to the same thing: a credit score worse than you already have. Prepare to hang up before agreeing to either of these terms.

The last thing you need to do before calling the creditor is prepare an agreement for a letter of deletion (see the two-page "Letter of Deletion" form found at WWW.7STEPSTO720.COM/FORMS or in APPLYING THE 7 STEPS TO A 720 CREDIT SCORE WORKBOOK). After all, you would not want the creditor to promise to provide a letter of deletion, only to have it back out on its word once you have sent the check. Have the two-page agreement ready to fax to the creditor immediately. Though the creditor might require the information in writing through regular snail mail, everything will move much faster if you can rely on fax machines or e-mail accounts to execute the agreement.

When you are ready to call the creditor, it is important to remember to remain calm. Upon calling the creditor, immediately log the name of the credit representative and begin using your script to guide the conversation. Stay in control of the conversation. Remember that you are offering only one thing, a payment (the amount you've already decided upon), and only in exchange for a letter of deletion. Nothing else will help your credit.

Do not:
- ❖ Get angry
- ❖ Let the creditor engage you in conversation about your priorities (or lack thereof)
- ❖ Let the creditor engage you in conversation about your responsibilities to pay back your debt
- ❖ Agree to a payment plan other than the one you have already decided upon
- ❖ Make any payment without receiving a letter of deletion

Finally, and most important, do not admit that the debt is yours. This is crucial for two reasons. First, in some states, an admission can restart the statute of limitations dictating the deadline for the creditor to sue you. Second, you are not likely to get a letter of deletion if you admit that the debt is yours. Avoiding admission will be a little tricky. You will have to work on saying things like, "I'm calling about account 123-456-789," rather than, "I'm calling about my delinquent debt."

If the credit representative is not willing to work with you, politely thank him and hang up immediately. Try another day with another credit representative.

If the creditor is willing to accept your terms, make sure you get a letter from the creditor agreeing to provide a letter of deletion to the credit bureaus once you have paid the amount you have agreed to pay. You can send the two-page agreement for a letter of deletion to the creditor, or you can mail copies to the creditor. Whatever you do, do not send a check without first receiving a signed agreement that the creditor will provide a letter of deletion.

When you have the signed agreement in hand, send a check immediately, along with a copy of the signed agreement, as well as the "Letter to Send with Payment 2" form found in APPLYING THE 7 STEPS TO A 720 CREDIT SCORE WORKBOOK or at WWW.7STEPSTO720.COM/FORMS.

On the back of your check, write the following: "By cashing this check, you agree that account number [insert your account number] is paid in full and you agree to provide a letter of deletion." This is called a "restrictive endorsement," and different states have different laws regarding the use of restrictive endorsements, so review your state laws or consult with a credit specialist or attorney before relying on a restrictive endorsement.

Make a copy of the front and back of your check for your records. Send the checks and forms through certified mail, return receipt requested.

Follow up as soon as you have proof that the check has been received. Request that the creditor send the letter of deletion immediately.

If the creditor does not send the letter of deletion, you should hire an attorney. The creditor has breached the agreement. Likely, upon receiving one letter from your attorney, the creditor will immediately provide the letter of deletion.

Negotiating with the Collection Company

Only negotiate with the collection company if the original creditor has charged-off the debt. Because collection companies are infamous for keeping poor records, some borrowers can have a collection item removed simply by asking the collection company to verify that the debt belongs to the borrower. This course of action is similar to the process described in

STEP 5 for removing errors. In short, you should send a letter (see the "Verification" form letter found at **WWW.7STEPSTO720.COM/FORMS** or in the accompanying **APPLYING THE 7 STEPS TO A 720 CREDIT SCORE WORKBOOK**) asking the collection company to verify that the debt is yours and that it properly belongs in collection. So long as the collection company does not deem the request frivolous, it is obligated to investigate your request. However, the collection company does not need much proof to verify the debt. Confirmation from the original creditor that the debt belongs to you and has lawfully and justly been sent to collection is sufficient to provide verification, so you likely will have little (if any) success with the verification process.

If the collection company cannot verify the debt, the collection (but not the original delinquent payments or creditor's original charge-off) will be suppressed from your credit report. See **WWW.7STEPSTO720.COM/FORMS** or **APPLYING THE 7 STEPS TO A 720 CREDIT SCORE WORKBOOK** for the "Lack of Verification" and "Lack of Verification 2" form letters and corresponding instructions. Remember that a suppressed item can reappear anytime on your credit report once the collection agency is able to verify that the debt rightfully belongs to you and in collection.

If the collection company does verify the debt (and it likely will), follow a similar process to the one you followed when negotiating with the creditor. Be prepared for the collection company representative to be an even nastier person than the representative of the original creditor. Unlike creditors, collection company representatives are often mean and will not necessarily soften as the conversation progresses. This means you will probably need to be more persistent. With a little luck, you will eventually find a representative that will be willing to settle on your terms.

Once the representative agrees to your terms, be sure you get a letter from the collection company agreeing to provide a letter of deletion upon payment of the amount agreed upon. You can fax the two-page agreement (see the "Letter of Deletion 2" form found in **APPLYING THE 7 STEPS TO A 720 CREDIT SCORE WORKBOOK OR** at **WWW.7STEPSTO720.COM/FORMS**) to the collection company, or you can mail copies. Whatever you do, do not send a check without first receiving an agreement that the collection company will provide a letter of deletion.

When you have the signed agreement in hand, send a check immediately, along with a copy of the agreement, as well as the "Letter to Send with Payment 2" form found at **WWW.7STEPSTO720.COM/FORMS** or in **APPLYING THE 7 STEPS TO A 720 CREDIT SCORE WORKBOOK**. On the back of your check, write the following: "By cashing this check, you agree that account number [insert your account number] is paid in full and you agree to provide a letter of deletion." (Remember that state law varies regarding restrictive endorsements. You should consult with an attorney to determine the laws in your particular state.) Make a copy for your records. Send the checks and forms through certified mail, return receipt requested.

What if the Collection Company Won't Sign the Agreement to Provide a Letter of Deletion?

If a collection company is caught providing letters of deletion to people who owe money, it will go out of business. This is one of the reasons I recommend that you refrain from admitting a debt is yours. It also explains why many collection companies might be reluctant to sign an agreement stating that they will provide a letter of deletion. Creditors and credit bureaus disallow this behavior, so if you get a verbal agreement from a representative who refuses to sign a physical agreement, you might want to take your chances, pay the account (be sure to write a restrictive endorsement on the check), and hope that the representative keeps his word. You might want to ask the representative if he will note the account accordingly; then, before sending the payment, call the collector, speak with a different representative, and confirm that the letter of deletion will be provided once the company receives payment from you.

Still Unable to Negotiate
for a Letter of Deletion?

Many attorneys suggest that you initially refrain from admitting a debt is yours, in part because an admission of guilt often restarts the statute of limitations on when a creditor can sue you. However, if you have been unable to procure a letter of deletion without admitting that the debt is yours, consider calling the creditor/collection agency and using a different recourse, but only after consulting with a credit specialist or attorney.

As I previously mentioned, collection companies are not technically allowed to "sell" letters of deletion to borrowers by trading a letter of deletion for a partial or full payment (though many will break the rules). If the collection company with which you are negotiating is unwilling to provide a letter of deletion, try offering an explanation as to why you did not know about the debt. For instance, if you have a joint credit card with an ex-spouse, who promised to pay the bill after the divorce, you could argue that you would have paid the debt had you known about it. A collection company is allowed a certain amount of discretion, so if you can, provide a genuine reason as to why you did not know about the debt prior to it being turned over for collection. If you can convince the collection company that you honestly would have paid the debt in full had you known in advance, the collection company will have the authority to furnish a letter of deletion.

If you still are unable to obtain a letter of deletion, you have several choices: pay the debt in full immediately, wait to pay the debt in full, make payments on the debt, or refuse to pay the debt. Let's go through the pros and cons of these options one at a time.

Option A: Immediately pay the collection item

Pros

❖ You will satisfy your agreement with the creditor.

❖ Your credit will be only minimally affected two years after the payment.

❖ If the collection is relatively new, your credit score is suffering regardless, so paying now will not significantly lengthen the amount of time your score suffers.

❖ Creditors/collection companies will stop calling you, and you won't be sued for failing to pay the debt.

Cons

❖ You will not be able to negotiate for a letter of deletion in the future.

❖ You might not qualify for low interest rates for at least two years.

When to choose this option

If you are not planning on making a large purchase in the next two years, this might be the best bet for you, especially if the collection activity is relatively new. Be sure to pay the debt in full as soon as possible so that your credit can begin rebounding immediately.

Option B: Wait for the "right time" to pay the collection item.

Pros

❖ You will eventually satisfy your agreement with the creditor.

❖ Your credit will be only minimally affected two years after the payment.

❖ If the collection activity is older than two years, waiting to pay the debt will allow you to delay the damage until you have purchased your home or auto.

❖ You might be able to negotiate for a letter of deletion down the road.

Cons

❖ You will prolong the suffering. If you wait to pay the debt, your credit score will drop in the future. Once you pay the debt, your credit will likely be damaged for at least two additional years.

❖ Creditors/collection companies will continue to contact you requesting payment, and you might be sued for failing to pay the debt.

When to choose this option

If you are planning on making a large purchase in the next two years, this might be the best bet for you, especially if the collection activity is relatively old.

Option C: Make payments on the collection item
Pros

❖ You will eventually satisfy your agreement with the creditor.

❖ You will likely be able to negotiate a payment plan, thereby stopping the creditor/collection companies from calling you and from suing you.

❖ If you do not negotiate for a payment plan, creditor/collection companies will continue to call you and you might be sued.

Cons

❖ **This is the most damaging option.** Your credit will not begin to significantly rebound for two years after you have paid the debt in full.

When to choose this option

If you have a problem saving money, and you feel obliged to satisfy your agreement with the creditor, this might be the best option for you, but only if you are not planning on making a large purchase anytime soon.

Option D: Refuse to pay the collection item
Pros

❖ Your credit will only nominally be affected four years from your last payment, and it will begin to improve significantly as early as two years after your last payment.

❖ You may be able to negotiate for a letter of deletion down the road.

Cons

❖ You will never satisfy your agreement with the creditor.

❖ Creditors/collection companies will continue to contact you, and you might be sued for failing to pay the debt.

When to choose this option

I do not suggest this option. Paying your debt is your responsibility. It is the right thing to do. That said, if you do not suffer from a crisis of conscience, you might choose this alternative if the collection activity is relatively old (two or more years) and you do plan on making a large purchase in the future.

Ultimately, the decision is yours. If you still are having problems determining when and whether to pay bills in collection, call **7 STEPS** at **(877) 720-SCORE** for a referral to a credit specialist. I highly suggest contacting an attorney or other specialist. Negotiating for a letter of deletion is a tricky art coupled with ever-changing laws and regulations. You would be wise to enlist the help of a specialist.

Preventing an Account in Collection from Being Reported to the Bureaus

Obviously, the best way to stop a collection from appearing on your credit report is to pay the bill on time. However, borrowers have another available recourse.

Upon being notified that an account is being submitted for collection, a borrower can immediately ask that the collector verify the debt. For instance, let's imagine that you receive a notice alerting you that your Sears® credit account is being sent to a collection company. However, you do not recall using your Sears® card. Within 30 days of the initial notice, you can ask the collection company to investigate the debt by providing a letter (please see "Verification" form letter found in the accompanying APPLYING THE 7 STEPS TO A 720 CREDIT SCORE WORKBOOK or at WWW.7STEPSTO720.COM/FORMS). Your letter should provide specifics as to why you do not believe this debt is yours.

Upon receipt of the letter, the collection company cannot report the debt to the credit bureaus until it has verified that the debt belongs to you. The key is to submit the dispute within 30 days of the initial letter. By opening a dispute, you stop two things from happening: 1) the collection company must cease all collection activity; and 2) the collection company cannot report your debt to the credit bureaus.

Of course, if the debt does belong to you, the collection company eventually will verify the debt, resume collection activity, and report to the credit bureaus.

Know the Law

Legally, you owe a debt until it is paid, settled, or wiped out in bankruptcy, and companies can sue you for failing to pay. The statute of limitation for such a lawsuit varies from state to state. That's right, lawsuit. If your collection account is less than $2,000, it is unlikely you will be sued, but don't take my word for it. Some of my more cautious readers might elect to consult an attorney who can determine the statute of limitation for their respective debt. If you are within the statute of limitation, you might want to simply pay the debt, regardless of its age. You should first try for the letter of deletion. It can't hurt, and it might mean the difference between poor credit and great credit.

When dealing with collection companies, you will notice that some of their representatives are nasty people. It is helpful to know your rights so that you can insist they not be violated.

Collections companies must:

❖ Call your house only between the hours of 8 a.m. and 9 p.m.

❖ Respect your right to be contacted in writing only if you so request.

❖ Stop contacting you at work if you so request.

❖ Be honest. They can't trick you into returning their phone call by leaving dishonest messages.

Collection and Home Loans

Some banks will insist you pay your accounts in collection before giving you a home loan. You should still try to negotiate for the letter of deletion. However, you might not be able to persuade the creditor to provide the letter in time. If this is the case, pay the collection item in full and be done with it.

As you know, paying your collection will damage your credit, and the last thing you want to do is hurt your credit before a large purchase. What if the lender decides to pull your credit report again and sees that your score has dropped? To avoid this, pay your collection at the close of escrow. This way, you will preserve your credit score until the last possible minute, and you will satisfy the bank's request.

KEY POINTS

STEP 6: NEGOTIATE FOR A LETTER OF DELETION BEFORE PAYING A BILL THAT IS IN COLLECTION.

Paying off a credit card after it has been in collection might further damage your credit. Bills that have been turned over for collection affect your score only minimally after two years and are all but erased after four years. Collection notices do remain on your credit report, but they affect your credit score only slightly. However, each time you make a payment on a bill in collection, your credit score will be damaged, and it will extend the amount of time the item stays on your credit report.

If you have a bill that has been in collection, you should not pay it until you get an agreement from the creditor or collection company to submit a letter of deletion to the credit bureaus asking that the derogatory item be wiped from your credit report. When negotiating for this letter, you should never admit that the debt belongs to you.

If you have items in collection, **STEP 6** is extremely important, so be sure to read it in its entirety. Also enlist the help of an attorney or credit specialist. For a referral, visit **WWW.7STEPSTO720.COM**.

step 7

Create a Structured Plan
to Protect Your Credit

As discussed previously, your credit report changes daily, if not hourly. Once you have started to build good credit, you will need a plan for maintaining it. Otherwise, your good credit can very quickly turn into bad credit. In fact of all the steps, this is the most important.

Once you have completed **Step 1** through **Step 6**, develop a plan to maintain your credit. To do so:

- Create a budget
- If in debt, live like a rich person (that is, be frugal!)
- Use technology to keep your bills current
- Review your credit card bills and bank statements monthly
- Pull your credit report at least once every six months
- Use the same name when applying for credit
- Avoid being a cosigner
- Keep your accounts active
- Protect your credit during and after a divorce
- If married, establish credit separately
- Review the **7 Steps** regularly

Create a Budget

If you find that you do not have enough disposable income each month to pay off your credit cards or invest in savings, you should create a budget. By creating a budget, you will identify where you need to cut back on spending. You will also stop making the impulse buys that might have ratcheted up your credit card balances in the past.

To create a budget most effectively, start by keeping a spending log. For one week, use the "Log" form (found in **Applying the 7 Steps to a 720 Credit Score Workbook** or on our website at **www.7StepsTo720.com/forms**) to write down everything you spend, down to the penny. You might not want to write down that 75¢ you use each day to feed the parking meter, but it adds up to $273.75 each year. Write it down!

KAREN

Karen, 33, is a hardworking attorney who lives in Los Angeles. She wakes up each morning at 6, drinks a glass of water, and runs to the gym, where she spends an hour. Let's take a look at her spending habits on just one day.

On the way home from the gym, Karen stops at a coffee shop and treats herself to a latte. She goes home, showers, and leaves for work. On the way to work, she stops to grab breakfast at a fast food restaurant. The drive-through line is longer than usual, so Karen is late for work.

She rushes through the first half of the workday, excited about her regularly scheduled lunch with her best friend, Maria. Because she came in late, Karen is running a little behind, so she drives to their lunch appointment instead of making the 10-minute walk that she takes on less-hectic days. At lunch, she orders a salad, bowl of soup, and an iced tea. She and Maria then share a slice of their favorite dessert: apple pie.

Karen drives back to the office and returns to work. At about 3 p.m., her energy level starts to crash, so she buys a soda pop and a bag of chips from the vending machine. She works until 7 p.m. and then drives to a restaurant to meet her boyfriend for a steak dinner and drinks. Afterward, they go to a late movie, where Karen buys a bottle of water.

Aside from the nutritional objection I have to Karen's diet, I have some financial objections. Let's look at what Karen's meals cost:

LOG OF DAILY MEALS

Items	Daily Cost	Yearly Cost
Coffee	$3.75	$975
Breakfast	$4.50	$1,170
Drink	$2.00	$520
Salad	7.00	$1,820
Soup	$4.50	$1,170
Dessert	$3.00	$780
Soda	0.75	$195
Chips	$0.60	$156
Dinner	$17.00	$4,420
Wine/Drinks	$12.00	$3,120
Water	$2.00	$520
Snacks	$3.00	$780
TOTAL	**$60.10**	**$15,626**

Yearly cost calculated as five days a week X 52 weeks

Assuming Karen spends only $50 a day on food, five days a week, 52 weeks a year, she's spending $13,000 a year on food. Even if she only spends $25 a day, she's spending $7,000 a year on food, which is more than $500 a month. Add in parking (she drove to lunch and to the movie theater) and entertainment, and she is spending another $2,860. And this does not include rent, car payment, insurance, gas, her gym membership, or any of the other expenses most people face.

You might think Karen's example is extreme. You could be right. She lives in Los Angeles, where the cost of living is high, and she is too busy to cook, so she eats at restaurants. The point of this example: most people are shocked at the amount of money they spend. This is why you should write it down. Perhaps you didn't realize that you were spending more than $25 a week ($1,300 a year) on coffee. Writing it down will force you to be conscious of your spending habits, and it will encourage you to stop making unnecessary purchases.

After you've written down everything you spend for one week, create a budget using the "Budget" form found in the **APPLYING THE 7 STEPS TO A 720 CREDIT SCORE WORKBOOK** or online at our website: **WWW.7STEPSTO720.COM/FORMS**. Your budget should list all bills and expenses as a monthly amount, even if they occur weekly or annually. For instance, if you pay taxes each year, you should estimate the annual amount and divide by 12 months to determine the amount of money you would spend monthly on your taxes. If you pay your babysitter weekly, you should multiply the weekly expense by 52 and divide by 12 months.

Start by listing the expenses you must incur. For instance, you need to pay rent, utilities, child support, etc. You also need to make the minimum payment on your credit cards. You must buy food and likely need health insurance. Next, you should list the expenses for things that are important to your quality of life ("important expenses"). For instance, if you live in Seattle, your gym membership might be crucial to your peace of mind. You cannot exercise outside because of the rain, so you spend $40 each month on a gym membership. Finally, list the "pleasure expenses." These expenses are those that you could live without. Perhaps you subscribe to a magazine you rarely read. Perhaps you treat yourself to a weekly massage. Refer to your spending log to determine what your pleasure expenses are.

You will now want to make sure that your monthly expenses don't exceed your monthly income. If you have more expenses than you have income, you should start cutting back on your pleasure expenses. You should also cut back on your pleasure expenses if your monthly income does not support paying more than the minimum balance on credit cards.

If you have cut all your pleasure expenses out of your budget and you still do not have enough money, you can consider one of two things: 1) cut back on "important" expenses; or 2) get a second job. One way or another, you need to make more money than you spend. When it comes to finances, it's better to be a realist than an optimist. I have a client who, for years, kept thinking her business was about to boom. It never happened, and she now owes thousands of dollars and has a poor credit score. I'll say it again: be realistic about your finances and how they relate to your spending habits. There's no two ways about it: if you spend more than you make, you will get yourself deeper and deeper into debt. Eventually, your credit will suffer.

For more information about digging yourself out of debt, see the next chapter, REBUILDING YOUR CREDIT.

If in Debt, Live Like a Rich Person

Countless Americans are in debt. We drive nice cars, live in nice homes, and eat well. We have a lot of available entertainment activities, and we spend money on clothes, books, gym memberships, and continued education. Some of us have satellite TV connections and TiVo® services, allowing us to be entertained any hour of any day. We pay people to clean our homes, water our gardens, wash our cars, and walk our dogs.

These are often the 15-minute millionaires—the people who spend extravagantly for a short while then find themselves neck-deep in debt.

But countless other Americans live less extravagantly. They drive older cars, live in modest homes, and buy only the essentials. They live on a budget, water their own gardens, and walk their own dogs. They save money on gas by walking or riding their bikes.

These are the true millionaires. Study after study shows that wealthy Americans tend to live less extravagantly. In fact, the people with the most money are often the most frugal. By refusing to keep up with the Joneses, they surpass them in savings and wealth.

If you cannot dig yourself out of debt, there is a good chance you are a 15-minute millionaire. You spend money as soon as you get it. You have expensive tastes and do not mind spending an extra $100 on a designer pair of jeans. But you should learn a lesson from the nation's wealthiest people: spend less than you earn and tuck some money away.

We all know how to do this: cut back on expenses. Cancel your cable. Bring your lunch to work. If you have a cell phone, cancel your home phone. Buy a reliable car instead of an impressive car. Make dinner instead of paying someone else to make dinner.

For some of us, this is easier said than done. If you are having problems, consider visiting Debtors Anonymous.

Others have experienced a tragedy, which has left their finances in jeopardy. Perhaps you have experienced a death or an illness in the family and your finances have suffered. If this is the case, you do have some choices, depending on how severe your debt is. Try negotiating with creditors. Remember that most people are kind. If you explain your situation, many people will want to help you. Perhaps you will get the creditors to drop your interest charges and late charges in exchange for full payment. Perhaps the creditors will defer your payment, or put you on a payment plan.

Use Technology and Automatic Payments to Keep Your Bills Current

Many banks offer online bill pay, which allows you to set up automatic payments online. Upon request, some businesses will automatically deduct your monthly payment from your checking account. Make use of these technologies.

Some people who struggle to master their budgets tell me they dislike automatic payments. After all, it stops them from withholding payment in favor of purchasing something else. These people are the people who need automatic payments most! If you struggle to pay your bills on time because you are too busy, or because you do not manage your money well, you should immediately set up automatic payment on all credit cards, mortgages, installment loans, and finance accounts. This will stop you from making other purchases instead of paying those bills that affect your credit. One way or another, you need to create a structured plan for paying your bills.

Review Your Credit Card Bills and Bank Statements Monthly

Each month, you will need to review your credit card statements to make sure that you are not exceeding the 30 percent utilization rate. You will also want to check the credit limit and the interest rate. If your limit has been lowered, you will need to adjust your balance accordingly. If your interest rate has increased, call the credit card company and inquire about the increase. You might also want to lower your balance even further. Though this might not help your credit score, it will help your pocketbook.

Review your credit card and bank statements and compare against purchases you have made. If you notice any unfamiliar items on your credit card statement or bank statement, you should immediately contact the credit card company or bank to determine if you have been the victim of identity fraud.

Pull Your Credit Report

Request your credit report and credit score every three to six months. The worse your credit, the more often you should pull your report. Upon running your credit report, review the 7 STEPS and modify your plan accordingly. Make sure that no new negative information has been added to your credit report. Also make sure that previously corrected errors on your credit report have not resurfaced.

Check for any indications that you have been the victim of identity fraud. For instance, look for unfamiliar names, Social Security numbers, and addresses.

Remember that you will not hurt your credit score by pulling your credit report yourself, so request it freely.

Apply for Credit Using
the Same Name

Always apply for credit and pull your credit report using the same name. If your name is Robert Michael Jones Jr., you might apply for credit cards under at least 16 different names:

Bob M. Jones	Bob M. Jones Jr.
Bob Michael Jones	Bob Michael Jones Jr.
B. Michael Jones	B. Michael Jones Jr..
Robert M. Jones	Robert M. Jones Jr.
Robert Michael Jones	Robert Michael Jones Jr.
R. Michael Jones	R. Michael Jones Jr.
Bob Jones	Bob Jones Jr.
Robert Jones	Robert Jones Jr.

Using a multitude of names when applying for credit is dangerous. It increases the risk of having your credit report information divided among the various names or even merged with another person's information (for instance, if you are Robert Jones Jr., and your father is Robert Jones, the credit bureaus might combine your files if you do not use "Jr." when applying for credit). Pick one name and always use it when applying for credit.

If you changed your last name upon marrying, start applying for credit under the new name. It might affect your credit minimally, but the affect is temporary; the new last name is forever.

Avoid Being
a Cosigner

BRETT

Like many young people, Brett ruined his credit at an early age. He simply was not financially responsible. Brett's main problem was that he was too optimistic about his future earnings. Everyone knows the type: Brett's next big deal was always right around the corner. He bought an expensive car, designer suits, and extravagant gifts.

After treating his friends to a meal at a five-star restaurant the night before, Brett showered and got ready for work. When he walked outside, he was alarmed to notice that his car was missing. He called the police, who told him that the car had been repossessed. Brett spent a fortune in taxicab rides over the next few weeks. Adding insult to injury, he found out that the bank still expected to collect money from him for the car because it had auctioned the car for less than he owed; the bank wanted Brett to pay the difference. Eventually, he had to buy a used car, which drained his small savings account.

Suddenly, Brett's financial situation crashed. All of his credit cards were turned over for collection. This was Brett's wake-up call.

He spent the next five years trying to dig himself out of debt, which he was finally able to do. He learned how to make and stick to a budget. He paid his debts and stopped making extravagant purchases. But his credit was so poor that he could not qualify for credit cards, and he knew he needed to have credit to get credit.

Embarrassed, Brett called his sister and explained the situation. His sister had always been responsible, so she was reluctant to open a joint account with her brother. He promised to pay the bill in full each month and use it for emergencies only. He explained that since she was a cosigner, she could monitor the account online. His sister finally agreed.

Brett's credit slowly climbed the first year. He qualified for a credit card of his own, albeit with high interest rates. After 18 months of timely payments, the interest rate dropped, and Brett qualified for another credit card, this one with an 8.9 percent interest rate. A few years later, he bought a new car at a low interest rate, and a few years after that, he bought a house. Over the years, he forgot that his sister had cosigned on his account.

Several years later, Brett was in a horrible car accident. He survived, but his credit did not. Brett had to quit his job. The loss of an income coupled with medical bills that insurance did not cover caused him to miss quite a few credit card payments. Brett was disappointed, but he had been through this before. He knew he could get back on his feet.

A few months later, interest rates fell and Brett's sister decided to refinance her house. When she came to me to refinance, she found that her credit had dropped 63 points since she first bought her house. Her chest tightened with anger as we reviewed her credit report. Her credit was spotless except for one item: the credit card she had opened with Brett years earlier.

Financial disputes can ruin relationships in an instant and are one of the leading causes of divorce. They can turn family gatherings, vacations, and holidays into tense and unpleasant dramas. And sometimes, unlike credit, the damage to personal relationships is irreversible. If you are not willing to take on the complete financial responsibility for the account holder's debt, do not go down this road.

Avoid being a cosigner unless you are willing to assume financial responsibility if the borrower cannot make the payments. In fact, when you cosign on an account, you become just as much of a borrower as the actual borrower. When you cosign on someone else's loan or credit card, your credit will be affected by all future activity on that account. If the person repays his loans on time, your credit will be affected positively. If the person is delinquent, your credit will be injured.

If you are already a cosigner, you should take the following steps to protect your credit.

- ❖ Insist that bills be sent to your address, or track the account online. This way, you can determine whether the borrower is paying on time. If not, you will need to make the payments on the borrower's behalf to protect your credit. To do so, make sure you pay a bill before it is 30 days past the due date. And, remove your name from the account (or insist that it be closed) the minute it becomes delinquent.

- ❖ More effectively, decide to pay the bill directly and have the borrower pay you directly. This way, you will always be in control of payment.

- ❖ Contact the creditor and see if the loan can be refinanced in the original borrower's name after a year of timely payments.

Keep Your
Accounts Active

Keep your credit card accounts active. It does you no good to tuck your credit cards in a drawer and never use them. Eventually, the accounts will show as inactive, and your credit might be affected. Remember: ideally, you need to have at least three active accounts to maintain a positive credit score. If you do not like having debt, consider paying a regular bill (e.g., phone or cable) using your credit card. Then pay it in full each month. This will preserve your credit and allow you to live without debt (and without paying interest).

Protect Your Credit
During and After a Divorce

Divorce is hard enough without suffering the extra burden of financial repercussions brought on by your former spouse. If you are going through a divorce, you should protect your credit by refinancing your home and canceling any joint credit card accounts.

RYAN

Ryan and Abby had been married for seven years. Like many married couples, they had joint checking and savings accounts. They owned a home together, and they owned cars together. Despite their two children, things began to deteriorate about four years into the marriage. They sought counseling, but their relationship continued to worsen. Eventually, they decided a trial separation might be the best course of action. Their temporary separation turned permanent, and they eventually divorced.

Abby immediately sunk into a deep depression, so Ryan and the children moved into a rented apartment together. Ryan was paying alimony, so he assumed Abby was able to pay the mortgage and her bills, despite the fact that she was not working.

One day, Ryan started receiving calls from creditors demanding that Ryan pay off his credit card bills. Ryan explained that he was divorced *and that his ex-wife had retained those accounts after the split. The credit card companies explained that the cards were still his responsibility. He owed more than $15,000!*

Ryan called Abby to discuss the situation. When she did not call back, he went to her house to discuss their options. When he walked in, he noticed that the house was a mess. A pile of unopened mail was sitting on the table. Ryan began sorting through the mail and noticed several letters from the bank addressed to him. When he opened the letters, he was shocked to find that the bank had started foreclosure proceedings on the house.

Ryan called the bank and explained that his ex-wife had kept the house after the divorce. Like the credit card companies, the bank did not care. As far as the bank was concerned, he and Abby were jointly responsible for paying the loan. The divorce decree and quitclaim deed might have changed Ryan's agreement with Abby, but they did not change his agreement with the bank.

Unless you want to be like Ryan, you will need to refinance your house in your name or in your spouse's name, depending on which of you retains ownership after the divorce. If your spouse retains ownership of the home without refinancing, your credit will be damaged if your spouse becomes delinquent on payments. Some people mistakenly believe that the divorce decree and quitclaim deed will rescue them from any repercussions if a former spouse becomes delinquent on his house payment. Unfortunately, the agreement you had with the bank remains in effect until your former spouse refinances under his name.

Some couples decide not to refinance because the spouse who retains ownership of the house does not think he can qualify for a loan without the other spouse's income. This is most likely untrue. Loans have been crafted to address this exact scenario, so protect yourself by refinancing. In fact, if you are going through a divorce, call **(877) 720-SCORE** for a referral to a lender who can help you find the right loan.

For the same reasons, you need to cancel all jointly held credit cards. To do this, contact the credit card company and inquire about its procedure for canceling an account. Your credit card company might require the cancellation request to be sent in writing. No matter what the procedure, it is important that you complete it quickly so as to avoid possible negative marks on your credit.

If Married, Establish Credit Separately

If you are married, try not to open joint credit accounts. Instead, establish credit separately and encourage your spouse to do the same. This way, you can leverage each other's credit when necessary. For instance, if you need a new line of credit and have a high utilization rate on a credit card, you can transfer a portion of your balance to your spouse's credit cards. You can then walk into the loan application with low personal debt and a higher-than-usual credit score. In other words, your spouse's credit score might be sacrificed for a short period of time so that you can obtain the best possible interest rate. If you or your spouse is a homemaker with little personal credit, this might be a difficult thing to accomplish. Call your lender to help develop a strategy and follow the **7 STEPS.**

KEY POINTS

STEP 7: CREATE A STRUCTURED PLAN TO PROTECT YOUR CREDIT.

Your credit report changes daily, if not hourly. Once you have started to build good credit, you will need a plan for maintaining it. Otherwise, your good credit can turn into bad credit before you can say FICO.

Once you have completed STEPS 1 through STEP 6, develop a plan to maintain your credit, as described below.

CREATE A BUDGET AND SPEND FRUGALLY. Make sure you are never late on payments and that you can keep your utilization rate below 30 percent.

USE TECHNOLOGY TO KEEP YOUR BILLS CURRENT. Set up automatic payments on all bills that you pay regularly. This way, you will never forget to pay these bills, and your credit will be protected.

REVIEW YOUR CREDIT CARD BILLS AND BANK STATEMENTS MONTHLY. Check the limit and interest rate and adjust your balance accordingly. Review your credit card and bank statements and compare against purchases you've made. If you notice any unfamiliar items on your credit card statement or bank statement, immediately contact the credit card company or bank to determine whether you have been a victim of identity fraud.

PULL YOUR CREDIT REPORT REGULARLY AND REVIEW THE 7 STEPS. Contrary to popular belief, if you request your own credit report, you will not hurt your credit score, so request it freely. In fact, the worse your credit, the more often you should pull your credit report. After receiving your credit report, review the 7 STEPS and modify your plan accordingly. Make sure that no new derogatory information has been added to your credit report. Also make sure that previously corrected errors on your credit report have not resurfaced. Check for any indications that you have been

KEY POINTS   continued

a victim of identity fraud. For instance, look for names, Social Security numbers, and accounts that are not yours.

AVOID BEING A COSIGNER UNLESS YOU ARE WILLING TO ASSUME FINANCIAL RESPONSIBILITY IF THE BORROWER CANNOT MAKE THE PAYMENTS. When you cosign on someone else's loan or credit card, your credit will be affected by future, but not historical, actions on that account. If you already are a cosigner, insist that the bills be sent to your house. This way, you can determine whether the borrower is paying on time. If not, make the payments on his behalf to protect your credit. Make sure that you pay a bill before it is 30 days past the due date. More effectively, decide to pay the bill directly and have the borrower pay you directly. Contact the creditor and see if you can refinance the loan in the original borrower's name.

KEEP YOUR ACCOUNTS ACTIVE. It does you no good to tuck your credit cards in a drawer and never use them. Eventually, the accounts will show as inactive. Remember: you need to have at least three major active revolving accounts to maintain a good credit score. If you do not like having debt, consider setting up an automatic payment to pay a regular bill (e.g., phone or cable) using your credit card. Then set up your checking account to automatically pay your credit card in full each month. This will preserve your credit and allow you to live without debt (and without paying interest).

PROTECT YOUR CREDIT DURING AND AFTER A DIVORCE. If you own a home or have joint credit card accounts, you will need to take immediate action to protect your credit during and after a divorce. When the courts decide who will retain ownership of your house, make sure the bank knows as well. Refinance your house in your name or in your spouse's name, depending on

KEY POINTS   continued

which of you retains ownership of the home after the divorce. If your spouse retains ownership without refinancing, your credit will be damaged if he becomes delinquent on payments. For the same reasons, you need to cancel all joint credit cards. To cancel these credit cards, contact your credit card company and ask for the procedure for canceling an account.

IF MARRIED, ESTABLISH CREDIT SEPARATELY. If you are married, refrain from opening joint accounts. Instead, establish credit separately and encourage your spouse to do the same. This way, you can leverage each other's credit when necessary. For instance, if you need a new line of credit and have a high utilization rate on a credit card, you can transfer a portion of your balance to your spouse's credit cards. You can then walk into the loan application with low personal debt and a higher-than-usual credit score. In other words, your spouse's credit score might be sacrificed so that you can obtain the best interest rate. If you or your spouse is a homemaker with little personal credit, this might be difficult to accomplish. Call **(877) 720-SCORE** for a referral to a lender who can help you develop a strategy.

preparing your credit for a home loan

When applying for a home loan, nothing is more important than your credit score. In fact, your credit score accounts for about 70 percent of your loan application. However, it isn't the only factor. Lenders will determine your credit-worthiness by looking at your credit, your income, your savings (both before and after closing the loan), and your down payment. But if you have a 720 credit score, some lenders might not consider your savings or your income at all! Remember, 720 is the magic number that will bring you one step closer to the American Dream: owning a home. Your credit score not only determines whether you will overpay on a home loan, it also determines whether you will qualify for a home loan.

If you are improving your credit so that you can buy a home, start the credit improvement process early. Ideally, you would start at least 24 months in advance if your score falls below a 620 and a year in advance if your score is lower than a 720.

Your first step should be to find a lender and ask him to pull your credit report. Remember that the credit score lenders see will not be the same credit score as you receive off the Internet. Though this will count as an inquiry, and will therefore impact your score slightly, it will give you the best assessment of what a lender sees when pulling your report. This will tell you how close you are to a 720 credit score.

If your score is lower than 720, ask your lender what this score tells him about your borrowing ability. If your lender doesn't suggest that you work to increase your score to 720, you have the wrong lender. Call **(877) 720-SCORE** for a referral to a lender who will help you use the **7 STEPS** to maximize your score and minimize your interest payments.

In addition to the **7 STEPS**, you will need to keep a few things in mind when applying for a home loan:

❖ Some lenders will ask your landlord to provide "verification of rent," or they will ask to see copies of your past 12 rent checks. Though your rent payments do not affect your credit score, they do affect your credit-worthiness. Lenders will look at the date on the rent check; if you have multiple late rent payments, the lender will consider you a high-risk borrower, even if you have stellar credit. For this reason, always write your rent checks no later than the first of the month, even if you do not plan on delivering the check for a few days.

❖ Certain lenders might deny you credit if you have hired a consumer credit counseling service. Though this does not affect your credit score, it does appear on your credit report, and some lenders see this as a red flag.

❖ Other lenders require you to pay collection items before providing you with a loan. If this is the case, pay the collection bills at close of escrow. Paying a bill in collection will hurt your credit score. Don't make the mistake of paying too early. If the lender decides to pull your report after you have paid the collection, you might not get the loan!

Afraid You Won't Qualify for a Home Loan?

SARA

Sara married her high school sweetheart, Tom. They had two beautiful children, and Sara was the perfect housewife. She was a member of the Parent Teacher Association, drove her children to soccer and piano lessons, and had dinner on the table when Tom came home from work.

Tom was an attorney who quickly made partner. With the money he earned, he and Sara were able to buy a large house with a swimming pool.

When Tom announced that he wanted a divorce, Sara was shocked and heartbroken. Aggravating matters, she didn't know what to do about an income. After all, she had never worked outside the home. Fortunately, because Tom wanted the divorce, he didn't put up much of a fight when Sara said she wanted to keep the house and the children.

Sara quickly decided to sell their large house and take out a loan to buy a smaller, more modest house closer to her parents. She would put the money she made from the sale of the home into savings, allowing her to go to college and earn a degree.

It occurred to Sara that she didn't have any credit. Everything was in Tom's name, including the credit cards, the car, and the house. How would she ever qualify for a home loan?

Qualifying for a home loan is getting easier and easier these days. Banks have loans for people with no credit, bad credit, stated incomes, and bankruptcies. Certain loans are designed for people who cannot document their income. These loans rely on equity and their credit score. Other loans provide sky-high interest rates and are designed for people with bad credit or no credit, like Sara. Call **(877) 720-SCORE** for information about these loans, and to be connected with a lender in your area.

Ultimately, Sara will qualify for a home loan, but she will not be pleased with the interest rates until she follows the **7 STEPS** and builds some credit.

Owning a home is one of the wisest investments a person can make. Creating a real estate legacy has allowed countless Americans with modest salaries to retire early, to send their children through college, or to make investments.

The fastest way to a home loan is by increasing your credit score and finding a wise mortgage broker. I'm sad to report that the recent refinance boom attracted a lot of mortgage "professionals" who are not educated about the industry. They put their clients in the wrong loans, and they do not pay attention to their clients' credit reports. They simply don't know the rules of the game: they fail to help their clients increase their credit scores; they run their clients' credit reports at the wrong time of the month.

And their clients suffer by paying hundreds or thousands of extra dollars each month in interest.

In short, they don't serve their clients.

To make sure that your lender serves your needs, call **(877) 720-SCORE** for a referral to a mortgage broker.

rebuilding your credit

I f you have bad credit, do not feel hopeless. Credit bureaus care more about your most recent behavior than they do about what you've done in the past. People change, and they recognize this. It does not mean that your score will jump after a few timely payments. The complete rebuilding process takes about five years (though you can qualify for a good home loan in two years if you follow the **7 STEPS**). If you have poor credit today, even if you have filed a bankruptcy in the recent past, you should have extremely strong credit and deep roots within five years of following the **7 STEPS**. Your credit will likely improve drastically in two or three years, but one thing is certain: you have to be very careful about your credit for five years, even if it seems to be repaired. If you make a late payment within five years of damaged credit, your score will suffer more than if you make a payment after five years of damaged credit.

If you are one of the many Americans who has suffered from poor financial choices, you might be inclined to wipe your hands clean, cut up your credit cards, and become a cash-only citizen. Resist this temptation: eventually, you will need credit, and no credit is just as detrimental as bad credit. Instead, start building your credit slowly. Get a secured credit card and eventually a few regular credit cards. Buy a car through a small installment loan. Pay your bills on time, follow the **7 STEPS**, and time will ease the impact of past mistakes.

If you need improved credit immediately, you can consider using a credit improvement company, which will work to improve your credit score on your behalf. Like consumer credit counseling companies, many credit improvement companies are run by scam artists. A legitimate credit improvement company will never promise results. Reputable companies are effective 70 to 75 percent of the time (most companies only have a 25 to 40 percent success rate). Others take your money, and then suppress items temporarily, only to have them reappear months later.

I also suggest that you ask a significant other, close friend, or family member to add you to his credit card account as an authorized user. So long as the account is in good standing, your credit score can be raised by having someone add you to an existing credit card account as an authorized user. A word of warning: if you are not careful, this strategy can damage not only your credit but also your relationship with the account holder. Additionally, if the account holder defaults or makes late payments, your credit score can be hurt (though not irreparably) because your name is attached to the account. Likewise, if you are irresponsible with the account, you can damage the account holder's credit score. To guard against this, the account holder might not want to give you an actual credit card. This is a win-win situation: your credit will improve (as long as the account holder is responsible with the card), and the account holder's score will be protected because you will not have a means of making purchases.

If you are listed as an authorized user on an account that is damaging your score (e.g., the user has made late payments or defaulted), call the creditor immediately and ask to be removed. This will eliminate the account from your credit report within 45 days, meaning the account history will not appear on your credit report and will therefore not impact your score.

Digging Yourself Out of Debt

Like a lot of people, you might be saying to yourself, *I can't pay my bills, much less start thinking about lowering my utilization rate, buying a car, and negotiating for a letter of deletion in exchange for a payment in full on my collection accounts!*

I can assure you that you are not alone, and you have choices. Though you should try to find other ways to dig yourself out of debt (such as getting a second job or negotiating with your creditors to temporarily defer your payments), you might want to consider bankruptcy or consumer credit counseling services, both of which can severely damage your credit. However, you might need to take these steps to wipe the slate clean, allowing you to focus on rebuilding your credit.

Bankruptcy

If your bills are too hefty to be paid back on time, you might want to consider bankruptcy. I know what you are thinking: *bankruptcy* is an ugly word. But declaring bankruptcy puts an end to it. As embarrassed as you might be now, you will have a fresh start once you have declared bankruptcy. Yes, it will hurt your credit, but if you are too deep in debt to get yourself out within the next five years, your credit will probably be trashed anyway from all the collection and charge-offs you are bound to face.

Bankruptcy, which was established to give people a fresh start, takes two forms: Chapter 7 bankruptcy and Chapter 13 bankruptcy. Under Chapter 7 bankruptcy, your assets are traded for your debt. That is, any nonexempt assets you have will be seized, but many of your debts will be wiped out. Exempt assets vary from state to state, but might include retirement accounts and home equity up to a certain amount. If you own a car, jewelry, or a home, you might lose them. You will not, however, lose the debt you owe for government-guaranteed student loans, alimony, child support, or taxes less than three years from the time of filing. You won't be able to discharge liens, though you will be able to get rid of judgments. As we discussed earlier, Chapter 7 bankruptcy will stay on your credit report for 10 years.

Under Chapter 13 bankruptcy, you will be allowed to keep your property. However, the court will create a debt repayment plan for paying off your debt within three to five years. If you default on this, either your bankruptcy will convert to a Chapter 7 filing, in which case your assets will be seized, or creditors will resume collection activities. Though Chapter 13 bankruptcy also stays on your credit report for 10 years, it is seen as more favorable to lenders than Chapter 7 bankruptcy.

Ultimately, you will need to decide for yourself whether bankruptcy is an option you want to pursue. It should probably be a last resort, and I strongly recommend against declaring bankruptcy if you want to increase your credit score.

That said, if you are considering bankruptcy, you should consult an attorney. For an attorney referral, contact one of our **7 STEPS** specialists at **(877) 720-SCORE**.

Be sure to tell your attorney that you do not want to list every account in your bankruptcy. Continuing to pay on one or more accounts will help your score rebound more quickly by telling the credit scoring bureaus that you did not use the bankruptcy as an excuse to erase all debts.

If you have already declared bankruptcy, do two important things as soon as possible. First, start establishing new credit immediately. You might need to open credit cards targeted to people with poor credit (e.g., secured credit cards). Lenders, especially mortgage brokers, want to see that the bankruptcy established a clean slate for you to become financially responsible.

Also find someone who will add your name to his account as an authorized user. Keep in mind that you should find an account that is in good standing with a low utilization rate. If you have declared bankruptcy, find an account that was established prior to your bankruptcy. The date this account was opened will appear on your credit report, and lenders will think that you kept this account in good standing despite the bankruptcy and therefore did not have it discharged during bankruptcy. This little trick gives lenders the idea that: 1) you were somewhat financially stable despite the bankruptcy; and 2) you did not use bankruptcy as an excuse to erase all debt.

Consumer Credit Counseling

Also consider consumer credit counseling. In this scenario, you hire a company to manage your finances. Instead of having you pay your debts directly and dealing with all of the phone calls from creditors, consumer credit counseling allows you to pay a lump sum to the counseling agency, which then disperses your money to your various creditors.

Legitimate consumer credit counseling agencies have developed relationships with lenders, allowing them to negotiate settlement amounts less than what was originally owed. This means your monthly payments will be smaller, and you will not have to deal with creditors calling your house all day.

Be wary of consumer credit counseling for a couple of reasons, starting with the scams. Unscrupulous businesses prey on people desperate to get out of debt. They ask that you send them a lump sum but then fail to disperse the money accordingly. The second reason to be wary is because consumer credit counselors do not always pay your bills on time or in full. Before hiring a consumer credit counseling service, ask how the money will be dispersed. Consumer credit counseling in and of itself will not hurt your credit score (though it is listed on your report and lenders might consider it a warning flag), but if the company is not paying your creditors, your accounts will become delinquent. You might not receive the creditors' phone calls, but you still owe the money, and your credit is still suffering if you do not pay on time.

forms
and worksheets

A copy of all forms mentioned in this book can be found in **APPLYING THE 7 STEPS TO A 720 CREDIT SCORE WORKBOOK**, the accompanying workbook, which can be ordered online at **WWW.7STEPSTO720.COM/BK**. Additionally, forms and worksheets can be downloaded at **WWW.7STEPSTO720.COM/FORMS**.

FORMS INCLUDE:

FORM 1	Incorrect Credit Limit Letter for Credit Card Companies
FORM 2	Incorrect Credit Limit Letter for Credit Bureaus
FORM 3	Letter Correcting Personal Information
FORM 4	Letter Requesting Addition of Personal Information
FORM 5	Letter Correcting Duplications
FORM 6	Letter Correcting Account Numbers
FORM 7	Mistakes in Your Payment History
FORM 8	Open Account Listed as Closed
FORM 9	Delinquencies Older than Seven Years
FORM 10	Collections Older than Seven Years
FORM 12	Bankruptcies Older than 10 Years
FORM 13	Request to Add Account
FORM 14	Request to Add Account 2
FORM 15	Correcting Information that Does Not Belong to Me
FORM 16	Resurfacing Letter
FORM 17	Resurfacing Letter 2
FORM 18	Script
FORM 19	Letter of Deletion
FORM 20	Letter to Send with Payment
FORM 21	Verification
FORM 22	Validation
FORM 23	Lack of Verification/Validation
FORM 24	Lack of Verification/Validation 2
FORM 25	Letter of Deletion 2
FORM 26	Letter to Send with Payment 2

Glossary

ALIMONY—Regular court-ordered, monetary payments made by an ex-wife or ex-husband to a spouse after a divorce is finalized.

ANNUAL FEE—The yearly fee billed by the credit card companies to the consumer for maintaining an account.

ASSET—The cash worth of anything you own, including property, possessions, savings, or investments.

AUTHORIZED USER ACCOUNTS—A credit card account set up in one person's name that has a card issued to another person so that he or she may charge against the account.

AUTOMATED TELLER MACHINE (ATM) CARD—A card that allows you to access the money you have in your checking or savings account. It is protected by a Personal Identification Number (PIN), which allows you to withdraw money and attain bank information from an ATM machine. ATM cards differ from credit cards in that they are secured by cash. When you use your ATM card, you are withdrawing money that you already have.

BALANCE—The total amount of money owed on a revolving account, installment loan, or mortgage. This total might include an unpaid balance from previous months; new charges from recent purchases; cash advances; and additional charges such as an annual fee, late fee, or interest.

BALANCE TRANSFER (OR "TRANSFERRING A BALANCE")—Shifting debt from one credit card to another, perhaps because another account offers a lower interest rate. Balance transfers are not always recommended as they can cause a person's utilization rate to exceed 30 percent.

BANKRUPTCY—A legal declaration of a person's inability to repay debts that discharges (or excuses) all debt, thereby stopping all actions by creditors against a borrower. Bankruptcy agreements vary but generally fit into two categories: Chapter 7 and Chapter 13. (See entries for Chapter 7 and Chapter 13 Bankruptcy below.)

BOUNCED CHECK—A check written without sufficient funds behind it. Also known as "a bad check."

BUDGET—A method of managing your finances that determines how much of your income you can apply to each potential expense.

CHAPTER 7 BANKRUPTCY—Under Chapter 7 bankruptcy, the court discharges most debts by selling the debtor's assets and property. Unless special provisions are arranged, the courts generally seize most property (cars, homes, furnishings, jewelry) under Chapter 7 bankruptcy. Chapter 7 bankruptcy, which appears on your credit report for 10 years, does not discharge any debts for taxes, child support, alimony, or student loans.

CHAPTER 13 BANKRUPTCY—Under Chapter 13 bankruptcy, the debtor and the courts settle on a debt repayment plan that allows the filer to keep his or her property so long as the debt is paid in accordance with the settlement. Though a Chapter 13 bankruptcy remains on a credit report for 10 years, it is less detrimental to a consumer's borrowing power than a Chapter 7 bankruptcy.

CHARGE-OFF—An account that has been sold to a collection company. In a charge-off, the original creditor no longer expects or attempts to collect any money for the debt. Instead, the collection company owns the account and is able to keep 100 percent of any money collected from the debt unless the debt was only temporarily assigned by the creditor.

COLLECTION (OR "IN COLLECTION")—The stage of an account after it has been delinquent for more than 90 days and the creditor has either enlisted the help of a collection company to collect the debt, or has sold the account to the collection company.

Collection Company—A company that collects debts on behalf of creditors. Also known as a "collection agency."

Consumer Credit Counseling Services (CCCS)—Organizations that try to help consumers pay their credit card debt. Consumer credit counseling services generally consolidate debts into one payment made by the borrower to the CCCS. The CCCS then disperses a portion of the money to the creditors. Consumer credit counseling can hurt a credit score by failing to make payments to creditors on behalf of the borrowers.

Cosigner—A person who agrees to be responsible for the repayment of a loan should the signer default.

Credit—Buying or borrowing now with the understanding that the debt will be paid in the future.

Credit Bureau—A privately owned, for-profit agency that collects and distributes consumer credit information in the form of individual credit reports. These agencies are subject to government regulations because of the sensitive nature of financial information. Experian, Equifax, and TransUnion are the three biggest credit reporting bureaus.

Credit Card—A card used to buy goods or services in exchange for a promise to pay the money over time. The borrower is responsible for interest charges that accrue if the balance is not paid off during the billing cycle, which is generally 25 days long. The borrower might also be charged an annual fee for the privilege of using the credit card account.

Credit History—The record of how a person has borrowed money and repaid debts. Also known as a credit record.

Credit Inquiries—Inquiries into a person's credit history that are recorded and become part of a person's credit history for two years. "Hard" inquiries are those made when a borrower requests credit from a creditor. Hard inquiries have a negative affect on a credit score. "Soft" inquiries are those made by the consumer or potential employer; they do not affect a credit score.

CREDIT LIMIT—The maximum amount of debt you are allowed by a creditor to accrue on a credit card.

CREDIT REPORT—A document that summarizes how you have paid, and continue to pay, your debts. This information is collected and stored by a credit bureau in a database and can be viewed by a creditor when a borrower applies for a loan or account.

CREDIT SCORE—The three-digit score given to a borrower by the credit bureaus. This score is based on a formula that predicts consumer spending behaviors and determines a person's credit-worthiness. (See FICO Score)

CREDITOR—A person, business, or organization that loans money to a borrower.

CREDIT-WORTHINESS—A creditor's measure of a consumer's past ability and future willingness to repay debts.

DEBIT CARD—A card used to buy goods or services or borrow money that is linked to an account with a bank in which the consumer has already deposited enough money to pay for the items charged. (See ATM Card)

DEBT—An amount of money owed to another person, business, or organization.

DEBTOR—A person who owes money.

DEFAULT—Failure on the part of a borrower to meet the terms of a credit agreement.

DELINQUENT—Late or overdue payments on a debt. Though a creditor considers a payment delinquent if it is not received by the due date, the credit bureaus do not consider payments late until 30 days after the initial due date.

DISCHARGE—Debts that are deleted during a bankruptcy settlement.

DOWN PAYMENT—The portion of the purchase price that the buyer must pay at present and cannot borrow from the lender. Often a percentage of the purchase price of a car, a home, or real estate.

EQUIFAX—Along with Experian and TransUnion, one of the three major credit bureaus.

EQUITY—Difference between the value of a property (i.e., real estate, a car, a home) and the amount owed on that property. For example, a $250,000 property with a $200,000 mortgage has $50,000 in equity.

EXPERIAN—Along with Equifax and TransUnion, one of the three major credit bureaus.

FAIR CREDIT BILLING ACT—A set of federal law that regulates how a creditor can collect debt.

FAIR CREDIT REPORTING ACT (FCRA)—A set of federal law that regulates the type of information credit reporting agencies can collect and disclose about consumers. The act was created to protect consumer privacy and ensure accurate reporting of financial information.

FAIR ISAAC—The company that developed the most commonly used credit scoring formula, called the FICO score.

FEDERAL TRADE COMMISSION (FTC)—The federal agency responsible for monitoring and regulating all issues related to credit and consumer affairs in the United States.

FICO EXPANSION SCORE—A method of determining the credit-worthiness of a borrower with little or no traditional credit history. Unlike the FICO formula, the FICO Expansion formula uses consumers' rent and utility payment histories to determine a credit score.

FICO SCORE—A statistical credit-scoring formula used by the credit bureaus to predict whether a consumer will repay a debt on time and in full.

FINANCE ACCOUNTS—A harmful type of credit that allows a borrower to delay payment on a purchase for more than 30 days. Finance accounts appear on a credit report as installment loans, and are the only type of credit that will always hurt a score.

FINANCE CHARGE—A percentage or dollar amount a borrower must pay to receive credit. The charge might include interest fees and/or cash advance fees.

FORECLOSURE—Legal action taken by a creditor to force the sale of property to satisfy a debt. Foreclosure occurs when the borrower has failed to make mortgage payments on a home. The borrower must vacate and the bank (creditor) sells the home to try to recoup the money borrowed.

HARD INQUIRIES—Requests for a credit report by a creditor. Hard inquiries negatively affect a credit score for one year but stay on a credit report for two years.

IDENTITY THEFT—Also known as "identity fraud," identity theft occurs when a person's personal information is used by another to obtain credit fraudulently.

INACTIVE ACCOUNT—Credit accounts that have not been used for a period of time, generally six months.

INSTALLMENT LOAN—A loan secured by property (e.g., a car or furniture) where the borrower agrees to pay the creditor the same monthly payment for a specified period of time.

INTEREST—A percentage of the balance that is charged by the creditor as a fee for borrowing the money or a percentage earned on money saved.

INTEREST RATE—The percentage of the loan that is charged to the borrower as a cost of borrowing money. Interest rates are determined by the lenders using the credit scoring system. The higher a person's credit score, the lower the interest rate.

JOINT ACCOUNT—An account that is equally owned by two people, usually a husband and a wife.

JUDGMENTS—A court order dictating the amount of money a borrower owes a creditor.

LATE PAYMENT—Defined differently by creditors and credit bureaus. For creditors, a late payment occurs when payment is made after the due date. For credit bureaus, a late payment occurs when payment is not made within 30 days of the due date.

LATE PAYMENT FEE—A fee charged by a creditor to a borrower when the borrower fails to make a payment on time. Late payments are generally about $29 to $39.

LETTER OF DELETION—A letter sent from a creditor or collection agency specifying that a derogatory item was incorrectly reported to the credit bureau(s) and should be removed entirely from a consumer's credit report.

LETTER OF PAYMENT—A letter sent from a creditor/collection company alerting the credit bureau(s) that a derogatory item has been paid in full, and that payment should be noted on the consumer's credit report. A letter of payment does not affect a consumer's credit score.

LIEN—Claims made against the property of another as security for money owed.

LOAN—An agreement between a lender and borrower whereby the lender gives the borrower cash and the borrower signs a legally binding contract to repay the debt.

MINIMUM PAYMENT—The least amount of money a borrower can pay to a creditor by a due date to keep an account current.

MORTGAGE—A loan secured by real estate. If the borrower defaults on the loan, the lender can take the property by which the loan is secured. Mortgages, if paid promptly, have the most positive affect on a credit score. If not made on time, mortgages can be the most detrimental to a person's credit score.

PERSONAL IDENTIFICATION NUMBER (PIN)—A "password" that is linked to your credit card, debit card, or ATM card and allows you to make transactions (withdraw or deposit money) on the account.

REFINANCE—To pay off an existing loan by applying for a new loan. Generally, loans that are refinanced have lower interest rates than the original loan.

REPOSSESSION—When a creditor seizes a piece of personal property (most often a car) to pay off a loan, or a portion thereof, secured by the property.

RETAIL ACCOUNTS—Accounts that provide credit to a borrower at one specific store or a chain of stores.

REVOLVING CREDIT—Credit that is extended indefinitely as a borrower pays off the balance.

SECURED CREDIT CARD—A credit card in which the borrower pays a deposit to the creditor to be used as security in the event the borrower fails to pay back the loan.

SETTLEMENT—An agreement between a borrower and creditor that solves or eliminates a dispute.

SOFT INQUIRIES—Requests for credit reports that do not affect the score. These inquiries are generally made by the consumer or by a noncreditor entity (e.g., a landlord or employer).

STATEMENT—The monthly bill from a credit card issuer that details the activity on an account. It includes the balance, recent purchases, recent payments, finance charges, interest rate, interest charges, and late charges accrued since the last statement.

STUDENT LOAN—An unsecured loan to a student through a bank or loan agency and guaranteed by the federal government to pay for college and related expenses. Student loans are one of the few items that cannot be discharged during bankruptcy.

SUBPRIME BORROWERS—Borrowers with credit scores under 620. These borrowers are considered higher risk.

SUPPRESSION—Temporary deletion of a disputed item from a credit report. Suppressed items are not used to calculate a credit score. Once verified as accurate, suppressed items will reappear on the credit report and become a factor in calculating a credit score.

TRANSUNION—Along with Experian and Equifax, one of the three major credit bureaus.

UTILIZATION RATE—The balance of a loan or credit line as a percentage of the limit.

**about
the author**

An expert in residential home financing, Philip X. Tirone is a mortgage broker and a major powerhouse in his firm's billions of dollars in loan sales. Philip has a distinguished background in difficult-to-obtain loans, having spent many years working with borrowers who had subprime credit scores. Philip has a unique ability to find loans for borrowers with bad credit, no credit, bankruptcy, and stated income. He has analyzed thousands of credit reports and works with his clients to maximize their credit scores to minimize their interest payments. His audio CD set and workbook, **APPLYING THE 7 STEPS TO A 720 CREDIT SCORE WORKBOOK**, were published by Nightingale Conant, the largest producer of self-development material. As well, he authored **7 STEPS TO A 720 CREDIT SCORE** and a seminar teaching borrowers how to prepare for a loan by improving their credit scores.

Philip created the ***Complete Financial Navigator*,™** a tool to analyze his borrowers' needs and financial picture, thereby helping borrowers overcome barriers to achieving their real estate goals.

The founder of the Los Angeles Educational Institute, Philip provides continued education to Certified Public Accountants. As a frequent guest lecturer at the University of California, Los Angeles, Philip has authored and delivered numerous speeches regarding the "Mortgage Lifestyle Dilemma," a phrase he coined to describe an emotional buying decision that results in overextension and a life that revolves around high mortgage payments. By analyzing industry-specific buying trends, Philip has devised a series of questions and answers to help borrowers avoid this dilemma.

Philip was named Arizona State University Man of the Year upon graduating with a real estate degree in 1994. Since then, he has continued to receive acclaim, most recently in the *New York Times* best-seller *Secrets of the Young & Successful*.